THIS MANUAL IS THE EXCLUSIVE
PROPERTY OF THE PRESIDENT OF THE
UNITED STATES OF AMERICA

_____

(Sign Here)
THE PRESIDENT

How to Be
President

How to Be
President

What to Do and Where to Go
Once You're in Office

STEPHEN P. WILLIAMS

CHRONICLE BOOKS
SAN FRANCISCO

Library of Congress Cataloging-in-Publication Data available.

ISBN: 978-0-8118-4316-4

Manufactured in the United States of America

Designed by Hotfoot Studio
Illustrations by Nancy Leonard
Typeset in Adobe Garamond and Franklin Gothic

Distributed in the U.K. by Hi Marketing
38 Carver Road
London SE2 49LT

A Quirk Packaging Book
www.quirkpackaging.com
10 9 8 7 6 5

Chronicle Books LLC
680 Second Street
San Francisco, CA 94107
www.chroniclebooks.com

Be courteous to all, but intimate with few; and let those few be well tried before you give them your confidence.

—George Washington, First President of the United States (1789–1797)

I once told Nixon that the Presidency is like being a jackass caught in a hail storm. You've got to just stand there and take it.

—Lyndon Baines Johnson, Thirty-Sixth President of the United States (1963–1969)

Contents

Introduction

Welcome to your first day as President of the United States.

The information contained within this manual is designed to assist you in navigating the many facets of your new position and is structured to advise and inform you regarding the most common situations you will encounter throughout your term in office. Through recurring sections of frequently asked questions ("FAQ"), essential protocols and skills ("Essential Presidential Knowledge"), essential tidbits of information ("FYI"), and significant facts of particular note regarding official functions ("Talking Points"), as well as dozens of "classified" diagrams and illustrations, you will receive basic guidance and instructions about living and working as president of the United States. Frequently used abbreviations are POTUS for President of the United States, WH for White House, FS for First Spouse, FF for First Family, and SS for Secret Service.

Versions of these pages have been passed down from and refined by every president since George Washington, and reflect more than 200 years of cumulative wisdom. Feel free to take notes on these pages, as you, too, will be called on to refine this manual before leaving office. It is advised that you carry this manual with you at all times during your first 100 days. Good luck, and God Bless America.

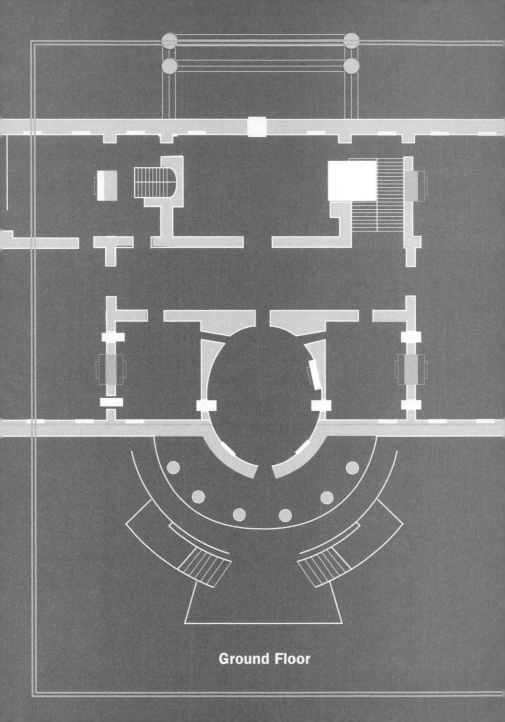

Ground Floor

CHAPTER ONE

GETTING SETTLED IN—
WELCOME TO THE WHITE HOUSE

The White House has long been referred to as "the people's house" of the United States of America. As president, you are invited—but not required—to reside here with your family (every president since John Adams has lived in the White House). In the last two hundred years, the executive branch of the government, which you head, has evolved into a White House–based institution. This live/work environment is well suited to the 24/7 nature of your job, allowing you to find downtime with your family, while remaining close to the important business of running the nation. In the White House, you will never be far from the situation room—or your bedroom.

Essential Presidential Knowledge
How to Order Breakfast

For room service, dial the operator to connect with your valet, or the White House kitchen. Breakfast of your choice will be delivered to your room or served at the FF dining table.

• Should you, members of the First Family, or any guests have special dietary considerations, such as food allergies, carbohydrate considerations, or taste preferences, please brief the White House Social Office. This office maintains a file on food needs and keeps the White House chef apprised.

- A sample breakfast menu:

Small glass orange juice
Two soft-boiled eggs
Broiled turkey bacon
Whole-wheat toast
Cantaloupe cubes

Coffee or tea
Butter and preserves
Milk
Sugar
Salt and pepper

Essential Presidential Knowledge
The Red Phone

At your bedside is a phone that will ring only in case of severe emergency. This is the phone your national security adviser would use to alert you to an attack on the nation.

- Everywhere you travel, there will be one phone line designated "red phone."

- It might be beige, black, or white, but its purpose will be clear: for you to receive and make calls in the midst of critical emergencies.

The red phone is not necessarily red.

Frequently Asked Questions

Do I make the bed? No, you do not need to make your bed, as the White House employs full-time housekeepers to complete this and similar tasks.

- If you desire that your bed be made in a certain fashion (for instance with the corners of the sheets pulled back, or with the pattern facedown so the folded edge reveals the sheet's print), please inform the head of housekeeping.

Where do I put my dirty pajamas? Hampers are provided in the FF bathrooms and dressing rooms. Please place all dirty laundry in these containers.

- Plastic bags and cards listing available services from hand washing to dry cleaning, similar to those found in hotel rooms, are located above the hampers in drawers.

Who does my laundry? The WH has laundry facilities and staff. The president and FF may deposit soiled clothes in any of the appropriate hampers, located in bathrooms and dressing rooms in the family quarters.

- The WH staff will take care of the logistics of dry cleaning, although the FF is responsible for paying the cleaning bill, which will be presented to you at the beginning of each month.

How do I get a haircut? There is no official WH barber or hair stylist. Presidents traditionally rely on the services of Washington, D.C.–area hair specialists.

- Whichever hair specialist you choose will have to undergo an extensive FBI background check and be cleared to enter the WH. For this reason, incoming presidents often have their hair styled by the person who coiffed their predecessor.

- The president pays for his/her own haircuts. Recent presidents have spent between $30 and $200 for their haircuts.

- Likewise, there is no in-house masseuse, manicurist, or facialist. However, these services are available from local providers.

Presidential Freebies

As president, you are entitled to a number of WH freebies and perquisites, including:

- Ballpoint pens
- Personalized stationery
- 64 TV channels provided by District Cablevision; unlimited channels via WH satellite receivers
- High-speed Internet access
- Toothbrush cups displaying the Presidential Seal
- Valet and housekeeping services
- Commander-in-chief terrycloth bathrobe
- Unlimited periodical and newspaper subscriptions
- All meals
- First-run and yet-to-be released movies, as well as older movies, provided free of charge by the Motion Picture Association of America
- Wake-up service
- Local and international calls
- Nightly bedspread turndown service
- Unlimited mints and hard candy

Deodorant, hair spray, toothpaste, and other personal, non-medical items are your responsibility.

Essential Presidential Knowledge
Your Family's Quarters

The following rooms and areas on the second floor are used as the FF's private quarters (note that the WH terminology is "ground floor," "first floor," and "second floor"):

- **The Ceremonial Stairway,** located just off the East Room, leads to the family rooms on the second floor. Traditionally, the Marine Band strikes up "Hail to the Chief" at the bottom of the stairs when you descend to meet your guests.

- **The Master Bedroom,** where you woke up this morning. While just yesterday your predecessor occupied this room, the linens for your administration are newly purchased.

- **The First Spouse's Dressing Room** is a small, sunny room in the southwest corner of the second floor, adjoining the Master Bedroom. (Many first couples have used this hidden spot as a private sanctuary.)

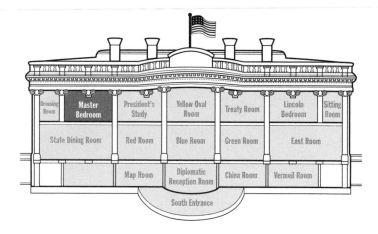

Second Floor

Main Residential Rooms

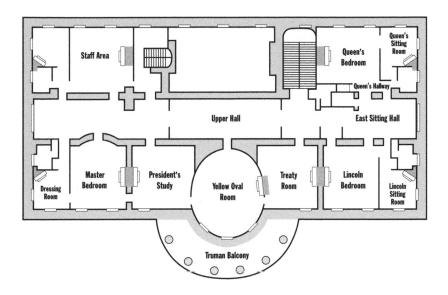

- The **President's Study** is where many first couples like to relax in the evenings. President and Mrs. Reagan often ate dinner from TV trays in front of the television.

- The **Yellow Oval Room** is the egg-shaped room with yolk-colored walls that opens onto the Truman Balcony.

- The **Truman Balcony**, a secluded balcony on the second floor of the south portico, is a favorite spot for presidential families to relax.

- The **Treaty Room** is where Cabinet members and other officials wait for the president when conducting business in the FF's personal area. Jacqueline Kennedy redecorated and repurposed this room in 1962, to "get the Cabinet out of my living room."

- **The Lincoln Bedroom** contains an elaborate 9-by-6-foot bed where President Lincoln never slept, but many guests do.

- **The Lincoln Sitting Room**, in the southeast corner of the mansion, is where many presidents read and relax. President Nixon smoked cigars there.

- **The Queen's Bedroom and Sitting Room** is a pink guest suite with a large four-poster bed. Queen Elizabeth of Great Britain, Queen Wilhemina of the Netherlands, Queen Frederika of Greece, and Queen Elizabeth II of Great Britain all slept in this room, which was christened the Queen's Bedroom in their honor.

- **The Executive Residence Dining Room** (not pictured) is where you will eat most of your meals.

As president, you may use any room in the WH at any time. However, the following rooms are often used by the FF to relax and entertain others:

- **The Library**, on the ground floor, contains 2,700 volumes pertaining to American life.

- **The Map Room**, on the ground floor, was used as a situation room by Franklin D. Roosevelt during WWII.

- **The China Room**, on the ground floor, is the only place in the world where the china patterns used by every U.S. president since George Washington are on display.

Ground Floor—Main Rooms

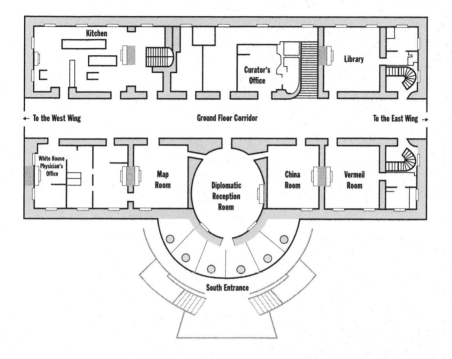

- The Vermeil Room, on the ground floor, displays the WH collection of vermeil (silver pieces dipped in gold), dating from the early 19th century.

- The Red Room, on the first floor, has red walls. The FF and guests often take tea here.

- The Blue Room, on the first floor, has blue walls. The oval shape of this room inspired the shape of the Oval Office, when the West Wing was constructed in 1902.

- **The Green Room**, on the first floor, has green walls. This room has been used variously as a card-playing room, a recital room, and an embalming room, for the eleven-year-old son of President Abraham Lincoln, who died of typhoid fever.

- **The East Room** is a large (2,844 square feet) empty space at the eastern edge of the White House that has been used variously as a gymnasium, a pen for General Lafayette's pet alligator, and a museum of Asian artifacts. More recently it has been used as a gathering place for presidential guests, and a venue for performances by musicians such as Kate Smith, Perry Como, and Harry Connick Jr.

Secret Passageways

- In the ground-floor corridor there is a door between the busts of Winston Churchill and Dwight D. Eisenhower. Enter that, cross the storage room, and exit near the florist. Follow this hallway until it forms an L. Make a right into a basement-like area until you reach a steel door, popularly known as the "Marilyn Entrance." This opens into a tunnel that passes under the East Wing of the WH and into the Treasury Building next door.

- On the second floor, there is a hidden door cut into the wall outside the Queen's Bedroom. This opens onto a staircase that leads to the third-floor solarium, from which you can enjoy the view of the night sky and Washington, D.C.

The White House

- Constructed in 1792 in the Palladian style
- Home to every president since John Adams
- Torched by the British in 1814, leaving only exterior walls intact. Reconstruction completed in 1817. North and South Porticos constructed in 1820
- 170 feet long and 85 feet deep (main section)
- 18 acres of land, 132 rooms, 6 floors/levels, 8 staircases, 3 elevators, 35 bathrooms, 11 bedrooms, 43 offices (including cubicles), 28 fireplaces, 147 windows, 412 doors, 824 doorknobs, 37 closets, 3 kitchens, 16 refrigerators, 40 sinks
- Handicapped accessible

White House Pet Policy

As president, you may maintain any pets you wish in the WH. Presidents usually have dogs and/or cats in their personal quarters, although a pony, a parrot, a goat, a zebra, and an alligator have been among the 400 pets kept over the years by presidential families.

- The WH staff will assure that animals are fed and watered, and walked when necessary. Any pet psychology or training services are the responsibility of the FF.

- Pets are allowed to write and publish books, although traditionally the proceeds are donated to charity.

- You may walk your dog, when desired. Otherwise, available members of the WH staff, including SS officers, your valet, and custodial staff will assume that responsibility.

Past Presidential Pets

- George Washington—dogs, several stallions, and a parrot
- John Quincy Adams—an alligator, presented to him by the Marquis de Lafayette
- Martin Van Buren—tiger cubs, presented to him by the Sultan of Oman
- James Buchanan—elephants, presented to him by the King of Siam, and a pair of bald eagles
- William Taft—a cow
- Woodrow Wilson—sheep and a ram that liked to chew tobacco
- John F. Kennedy—dogs, cats, a pony, a canary, hamsters, a rabbit, and a horse
- William Jefferson Clinton—a dog and a cat that became a best-selling author
- George W. Bush—two dogs and a cat

Ghosts in the West Wing

Many residents and visitors have encountered ghosts in the WH. These include:

- President Harrison's ghost, talking in the attic
- The spirit of President Lincoln wandering near his former bedroom (his actual bedroom—not the one named for him)
- The ghost of First Lady Abigail Adams walking through the halls, carrying an object in her outstretched arms or acting as if she's doing the laundry by hand
- President Andrew Jackson's ghost, in the FF's bedrooms

- The spirit of a black cat in the basement (most often seen just before major disasters, such as an assassination or stock market crash)
- The ghost of First Lady Dolly Madison, in the Rose Garden

The White House Gardens

- The two oldest trees on the grounds are Southern Magnolias that were planted by President Andrew Jackson between 1829 and 1837, in honor of his wife, who died before he was sworn in as president.
- The ceremonial Rose Garden was first planted in 1913.
- Apple trees and grapevines grow on the grounds.
- A Children's Garden, located just off the main portico, was planted by Lady Bird Johnson.
- Many presidents have planted a tree on the WH grounds. Late fall is the best time to plant a tree. There are currently 36 presidential trees standing.

Essential Presidential Knowledge
How to Get New Furniture

Contact the Director of the National Park Service, who is authorized to accept furniture donations or order new furniture for the WH.

- You may decorate to any extent you wish. Each incoming FF brings with it a personal sense of style and taste preferences, and the newcomers often request new paint colors, draperies, carpets, and other changes.

- In the past, these costs have most often been covered by private donations. The rules regarding furniture are outlined in the *U.S. Code Sec. 110—Furniture for the Executive Residence at the WH:*

  "All furniture purchased for the use of the Executive Residence at the WH shall be, as far as practicable, of domestic manufacture. With a view to conserving in the Executive Residence at the WH the best specimens of early American furniture and furnishings, and for the purpose of maintaining the interior of the Executive Residence at the WH in keeping with its original design, the Director of the National Park Service is authorized and directed, with the approval of the president, to accept donations of furniture and furnishings for use in the Executive Residence at the WH, all such articles thus donated to become the property of the United States and to be accounted for as such."

Frequently Asked Questions

What if I need a doctor? Different offices within the WH structure work together to keep you and the FF in good health.

- The Office of the Physician (OP) to the president offers worldwide emergency medical service and regular, comprehensive medical care to you and the FF.

- Working with the SS and the WH Military Office, the OP gleans unparalleled global medical intelligence, makes emergency contingency plans and performs lifesaving interventions when necessary.

- In addition to serving the FF, the OP will treat any WH guest who desires help.
- There is a fully equipped doctor's office in the WH basement.
- The federal government pays your medical and psychiatric bills.

Where do we park? For security reasons, you will not be allowed to drive your own vehicle except at remote locations such as presidential ranches and country homes.
- This also applies to the FS. First Children are allowed to drive, provided they maintain contact with the SS agents assigned to them.
- You may park up to three family vehicles in the reserved spaces behind the West Wing. It's best to notify the SS before leaving in your vehicle. President Gerald Ford's daughter Susan once raced her car out through the WH gate after the gate had been opened to let in another car. She quickly disappeared, causing consternation among the SS agents who were supposed to know her whereabouts and accompany her.

Where do I get stamps and cash? You may use your ATM card to obtain money, 24 hours a day, from the WH Credit Union Machine in the basement of the WH.
- You may purchase stamps, using the stamp machines, in the WH post office, also in the WH basement.

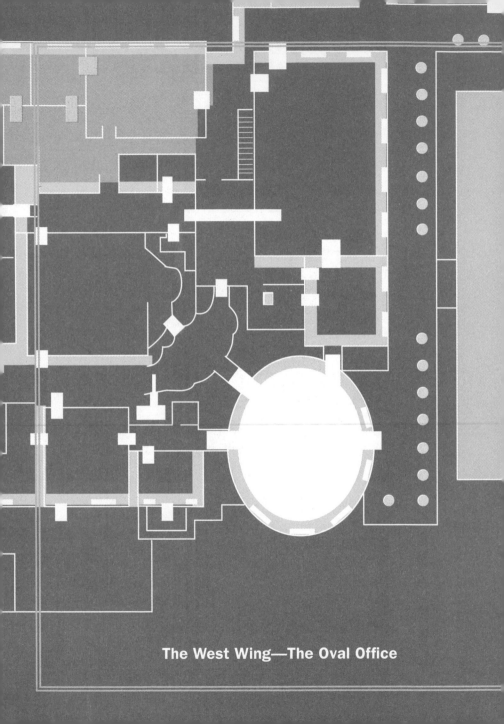

The West Wing—The Oval Office

CHAPTER TWO

GETTING DOWN TO WORK— THE DAILY GRIND

The presidency is often described as the world's most difficult job. Yet like any job, it is manageable when reduced to its basic functions. The Oval Office is, like any other office, a place where you work, play, strategize, snack, think and rest, doodle, and compose. The great thing about being president is that no one can tell you which of these functions to perform at which time of the day. As you start your workday in the Oval Office, remember that you are the chief executive, and as such, set your own timetable. While there are certain traditions you should respect and uphold, given the historical nature of your job, your veneration of the presidency needn't mean that you can't make your own imprint on the office. The most effective presidents have always made good use of delegating authority for tasks and trusting their staffs to ensure that the job gets done. No president has shoulders large enough to carry every burden. Since you have a staff of thousands, and a budget in the hundreds of millions of dollars, make use of the expertise at your fingertips.

Essential Presidential Knowledge
The Oval Office
The Oval Office is where you will confer with heads of state, diplomats, and other dignitaries, and is the site for broadcasting presidential addresses to the nation. Originally built in 1909, it was relocated to its current location in the West Wing, overlooking the Rose Garden, in 1934. The oval shape is intended to position the president in the center of the room, equidistant from all other people in the room.

The Oval Office

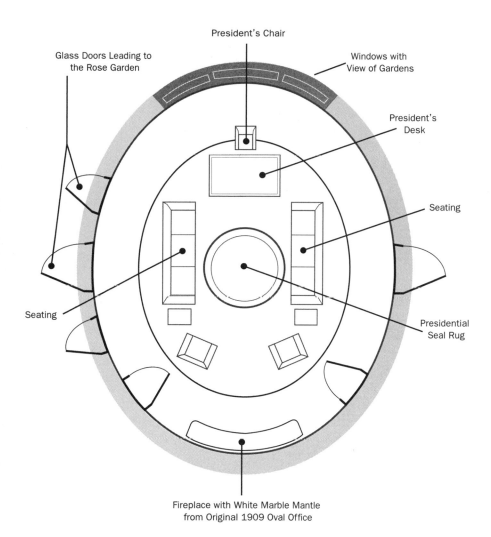

President's Chair

Glass Doors Leading to
the Rose Garden

Windows with
View of Gardens

President's
Desk

Seating

Seating

Presidential
Seal Rug

Fireplace with White Marble Mantle
from Original 1909 Oval Office

- Four doors serve the Oval Office: one to the hallway (walkway #2); one to the secretary's area; one onto the patio to the Rose Garden; and one into the president's study. The president's bathroom, the only private bathroom in the West Wing, is entered through the study off the Oval Office.

- The Oval Office is under very tight security, by SS agents and staff members. No one, including the FS, may enter the office unannounced.

The West Wing, First Floor

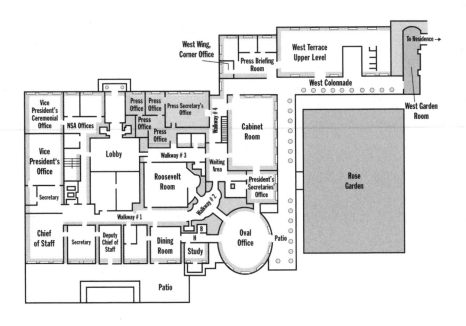

The West Wing

- The West Wing was constructed in 1902 by President Theodore Roosevelt as a temporary office, to make more space for his large family in the WH. It replaced greenhouses dating back to the 1850s.

- It has remained the presidential office wing of the WH and includes the Oval Office, the offices of the president's executive staff, including the Vice President, the Cabinet Room, the Roosevelt Room, and the James S. Brady Press Briefing Room.

- The president's office was originally rectangular.

- The Oval Office was constructed in 1909 by President William Howard Taft.

- Air conditioning was added to the West Wing after a fire in 1929.

- President Franklin Roosevelt called the Roosevelt Room the Fish Room, where he displayed an aquarium and fishing mementos.

- Franklin Roosevelt expanded the West Wing and built a swimming pool in 1934.

- President Richard Nixon turned the swimming pool into the press briefing room during his time in office.

- The Cabinet Room is between the Oval Office and the press briefing room, looking out on the Rose Garden. It is furnished with a mahogany conference table and leather chairs, each with a brass nameplate designating the cabinet member who sits in it.

- The patio, with its columns and tile floor, is where the president often relaxes on nice days.

The Oval Office Desk

Almost every president since Rutherford B. Hayes (except Presidents Lyndon Baines Johnson, Richard M. Nixon, and Gerald R. Ford) has used the same desk.

The desk was built from timbers salvaged from the HMS *Resolute*, an Arctic rescue vessel used by the British that broke up and became icebound near Greenland in 1854. When the ice broke, the ship drifted without crew for more than one thousand miles until discovered by an American ship, the *George Henry*, which took it to Connecticut. It was later returned to England, as a token of good will, where it served the Royal Navy for two more decades.

When the vessel was decommissioned, Queen Victoria decided to turn the wood into a desk for the president of the United States. The 1,300-pound desk was delivered to President Rutherford B. Hayes in November 1880.

Two presidents have modified the desk since then. President Franklin D. Roosevelt added the presidential coat of arms, and President Ronald Reagan lifted it onto a two-inch base to make it more comfortable for his 6'2" frame. It was exhibited at the Smithsonian Institute for ten years until President Jimmy Carter asked for it back.

You may, however, choose your own Oval Office desk from any in the WH collection.

Essential Presidential Knowledge
How to Get a Chair

While you may choose to sit in whatever chair you wish, at least nine recent U.S. presidents have used the Gunlocke brand Oval Office Chair.

- This model was designed in 1961 to ease President John F. Kennedy's back pain, with the assistance of his personal physician.

- The chair has sinuous spring suspension, based on 11-gauge steel springs running across the seat of the chair, foam no-sag seating, and a firm foam back over a spring foundation. The interior solid-maple frame is double-dowed, corner-blocked, and screwed for durability. It is upholstered in soft, top-grain, black leather.

How to Get a Rug

Following a tradition that isn't well-understood or well-documented, presidents are encouraged to design their own Oval Office rug with the aid of knowledgeable WH staffers. Most presidents choose a version of the presidential coat of arms and select a color scheme that blends in with their redecoration, if any, of the Oval Office.

- The rugs are produced by a private company, in 100-percent wool. Your staff will see that the rug is produced and placed in the Oval Office for the duration of your employment.

Your Pen

- Traditionally, Parker pens have been used by presidents to sign treaties and bills. At times, the president will sign copies of a bill, or different portions of a document, with as many as 15 different pens.

- The pens are then given as gifts to legislators, diplomats, and others as rewards for their contributions.

Presidential Hours

As president, you may work as little or as much as you deem necessary. Some presidents choose to be on the job every waking hour. Others take breaks and try to maintain a somewhat normal family life.

- President Ronald Reagan was famous for taking naps during the day.

- President George W. Bush would generally arrive at the Oval Office at 7 a.m., take a two-hour exercise break during the day, and try to leave the office by late afternoon.

- President Bill Clinton, on the other hand, was known for working all day and into the evening, and then working the phones from his private residence until 2 or 3 in the morning.

Your Official Job Description

The only duties specified in the Constitution are that of chief executive and commander in chief, yet other duties are assumed, based on precedent, legal decisions, and popular mandate. Your duties include:

- As chief executive, you enforce the federal laws, treaties, and federal court rulings; develop federal policies; prepare the national budget; and appoint federal officials.

- As commander in chief, you direct national defense and decide whether or not to use nuclear weapons.

- As foreign policy director, you determine U.S. relations with other nations, appoint ambassadors, and make treaties.

- As legislative leader, you recommend laws and work to win their passage in Congress.

- As head of your political party, you mold your party's positions on national and international issues.

- As popular leader, you inspire citizens to work toward achieving the nation's goals.

- As chief of state, you perform a variety of ceremonial duties.

How the President Gets Information

As president, you will be deluged with communications. A system of filters has been devised to ensure that all information is reviewed and either passed to you or forwarded to the right person for handling.

- Level 5: The average citizens across America who want to communicate with the president.

- Level 4: Staff Secretaries; mail delivery to president's "private zip code" used by his personal friends, politicians, and other important people who receive information to be passed on to the president.

- Level 3: The President's Personal Secretary; an aide; the Office of Presidential Correspondence.

- Level 2: The Director of Oval Office Operations (located outside the Oval Office "back door"): This person's job is to filter every piece of paper going into the Oval Office, to watch and make note of every person who enters the Oval Office (even the First Spouse needs this director's permission to enter the Oval Office), and to screen all phone calls. This director's most commonly used word is "no."

- Level 1: The Oval Office. The president at his desk.

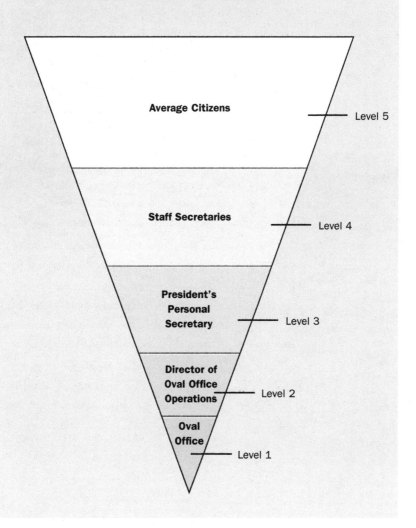

How the President Gets Information

Average Citizens — Level 5

Staff Secretaries — Level 4

President's Personal Secretary — Level 3

Director of Oval Office Operations — Level 2

Oval Office — Level 1

The Daily Brief

The president's first business of the day is the presidential daily briefing, which takes place early in the morning (no later than 7 a.m.) with the Chief of Staff, National Security Adviser, and, possibly, Secretary of State, as well as the head of the Central Intelligence Agency, or a representative.

- At this meeting any new threats, rumors, or other information gathered by intelligence operatives around the world is brought to the president's attention.

- In addition, each night the CIA prepares a 10- to12-page document called the President's Daily Brief. This three-ring loose-leaf notebook, embossed with the words "President's Daily Brief" in gold lettering, covers vital information regarding the previous 24 hours.

- Terrorist threats, health problems of world leaders, economic disasters, and other important news is covered in brief reports within the notebook.

- Normally, the director of the CIA and some of your staff, such as the National Security Adviser, will join you at an 8 a.m. meeting to discuss this document.

- Only 10 or so people are privy to the president's daily briefing, and CIA agents return all copies of the briefing to their headquarters in Langley, Virginia, after the meeting.

Frequently Asked Questions

How do I get mail? As president, you will receive around five million letters each year from citizens, friends, and commercial establishments. In addition, you will receive close to a million e-mails.

• All of these will be screened by your staff. It is recommended that you not have a personal e-mail account, because such communications are not secure.

• There is a way for you to receive personal mail. The United States Postal Service has assigned the president a private zip code, used by no other person or location in the country. Any letters addressed with this zip code will be delivered directly to your office.

• All of your mail will be opened by your secretary.

• Personal letters from family and friends will be bundled and given to you. Other letters will be summarized and brought to your attention as needed.

How do I get/make phone calls? All of your incoming telephone calls will be screened by your staff, which will also record all incoming and outgoing calls. Your secretary will dial all of your outgoing calls.

• Personal calls may be received on your private number.

• Citizens who want to reach you will be directed to the White House Comment Line, (202) 456-1111, which is staffed by more than one hundred volunteers and paid employees.

- Each week you will receive a report summarizing the several thousand phone calls you've received. The calls come from people with concerns ranging from a lost Social Security check to suicidal feelings.

- It is rare for a president to return a phone call from a member of the public. A staff member will either phone the person or send a letter suggesting a course of action or thanking that person for their communication.

- You may give your secretary a list of people who should have access to you, and their calls will be forwarded directly to your office. Otherwise, the decision on whether or not you are available will be made by your staff—primarily your secretary, but also your Chief of Staff and others.

Frequently Asked Questions

How do I get the news? The White House Communications Agency, WHCA, records most television news shows and will give them to you or your staff, on request.

- Most offices in the WH have television sets for watching this news compilation.

- In addition, your staff will give you a summary of the daily news from papers, magazines, and other sources.

- As necessary, you will receive intelligence briefings from the Central Intelligence Agency, the Federal Bureau of Investigation, and the National Security Agency.

• You may, at no charge, order subscriptions to any national or international newspapers and periodicals. Your staff can bookmark useful news sites on your web browser.

Essential Presidential Knowledge
The "Nuclear Football"

A military officer (the assignment rotates among the three branches of the military) will shadow you at all times with the "nuclear football" handcuffed to his wrist. This vital tool of national defense, which will never be more than a few feet from your side, no matter where you are in the world, can influence the future of life on earth.

• All the officers (who carry the rank of lt. colonel, naval commander, or Marine major, depending upon their branch of service) who work with the football must pass the highest security clearance. Known as

The 45-pound Briefcase

"Yankee White," this level of clearance requires U.S. citizenship, absolute loyalty to the country, and absence of any foreign influence over the officer, his or her family, and close friends. It is unlikely that a U.S. citizen married to a foreigner would have this job.

• The 45-pound briefcase allows you to respond with nuclear weapons to a military threat. Each morning the National Security Agency will issue a new set of codes that make the briefcase operational.

• You may store the codes in your wallet, or wrap them around your credit cards with a rubber band, as one president did. (It is not advisable to leave them in your suit pocket and send it to the cleaners, as another president did.)

Secure Satellite Radio

• In addition to the codes, known as Gold Codes, this briefcase contains a secure satellite radio and the President's Decision Book. The President's Decision Book has 75 pages of nuclear strike options that the president may consider, including Major Attack Options (MAOs), Selected Attack Options (SAOs), and Limited Attack Options (LAOs).

• In response to a threat from nuclear or conventional forces, you may choose to activate Launch on Warning (LOW) or Launch Under Attack (LUA).

President's Decision Book

Essential Presidential Knowledge
Making a Quick Escape

In case of an attack on the WH or another emergency, turn immediately to the nearest SS agents for guidance. They will take you firmly by the shoulders and guide you to the appropriate location.

• Do not argue or delay their actions, as they have a mandate to assist you before all others, even the FF.

- Depending on the circumstances, you could be led to the fortified bunker located in the basement of the WH, or to emergency locations in nearby buildings, including the Old Executive Office Building, accessible by a WH tunnel. For reasons of National Security, these locations will remain secret, even to you, unless there is an emergency.

- Several of these undisclosed (classified) fortified locations are within a short helicopter ride or drive from the WH. Others are located at military bases and other locations around the country, accessible by Air Force One. The plane itself is designed to withstand various types of attack, including fallout from a nuclear attack, and has the most protected and advanced communication devices available.

- During times of heightened threat, a "shadow" government, composed of high-level bureaucrats, operates out of safe bunkers in the Washington, D.C., area. The bunkers have generators, computers, telephones, water, and food. This infrastructure would be available to you in case of emergency. When the SS determines that the risk has subsided, you will be immediately returned to the WH.

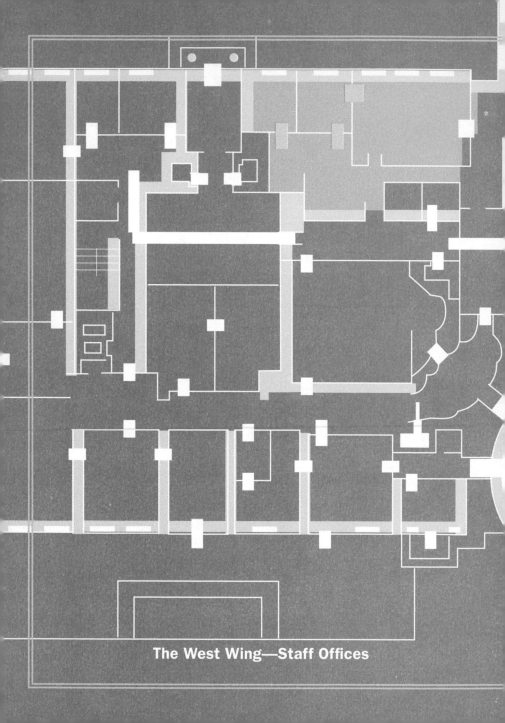

The West Wing—Staff Offices

CHAPTER THREE

GETTING TO KNOW YOUR STAFF— PEOPLE AND POSITIONS

A president's job is never done, and it is therefore important to balance the need for rest with the need to attend to business. Fortunately, the Oval Office is just a short walk away from the comfort of the Executive Residence, so you can easily remain in top form for tackling the business of running the country. There is no typical day for a president, and you may find yourself interrupting a meeting with the Prime Minister of England to take a phone call from your top general in the Middle East. Or a flight to Toledo, Ohio, to settle a labor dispute might require you to cut short your visit with the First Spouse in the Residence. As president, you must be prepared to adapt to any exigency. Since most of the mundane business of the day will have been taken care of before and immediately following lunch, the afternoon is a fine time to exercise, return personal phone calls, visit with old friends, and relax your mind for the evening hours. (That is, assuming that the events of the world allow you to take a little time for yourself.) Such is the life of the president of the United States of America.

Getting to Know Your Staff

Each incoming president hires a personal staff of more than six thousand people who work out of offices across the country. In addition, there is an institutional staff of the executive branch that is carried over from year to year.

• Most WH staff members work out of large, well-appointed offices in the Old Executive Office Building (OEOB), not far from the West Wing of the WH.

- Offices in the West Wing are usually small and window-less. However, most staff members would prefer cramped quarters in close proximity to the president to grand quarters in the OEOB. These staff members jump to their feet and stand whenever the president passes in the hallway. The core of the president's personal staff is composed of these offices:

Office of the Chief of Staff

The Chief of Staff oversees everything that goes on in the WH, and has only one boss: you. The Chief of Staff controls your schedule, decides who is invited to which meeting, reviews all papers that come in and out of the president's office, and accompanies the president on trips.

Office of the Staff Secretary

Every document for the president, other than highly classified information, passes through this office. The secretary reads the document and summarizes it for the president. The secretary oversees the Correspondence Office and the Office of Records Management. There is a secretary on duty every day from 7 a.m. until 1 a.m.

Office of Counsel

The WH Counsel attends important daily WH meetings and determines which issues or actions you take might have negative legal consequences. If necessary, the counsel refers decisions and issues to the United States Department of Justice for review.

Office of Scheduling

More than half the president's time is dedicated to events that the president has little choice but to attend, such as intelligence briefings and staff meetings. In addition, you will receive approximately one thousand requests each week for your time. The Director of Appointments and Scheduling makes sure that your days are spent productively.

Advance Office

The Advance Office coordinates all of the president's travels, including on-site media appearances, security, transportation, and scheduling.

Oval Office Operations

This relatively new office, which was created under President Clinton, supervises the president's personal secretary and other aides, and the Office of Presidential Correspondence. The Director of Oval Office Operations is seated at a desk just outside the Oval Office entrance.

Office of Presidential Correspondence

The hundreds of members of this office answer the millions of letters, faxes, and e-mails the president receives each year. The staff will select especially interesting examples of correspondence for you to read and reply to personally. The staff also composes presidential greetings to people on their birthdays, graduations, earning of Eagle Scout awards, weddings, and other important dates.

Office of Management and Administration

This support office manages the Military Office (2,200 military personnel serve the White House daily, using more than 46,000 pieces of state-of-the-art equipment), the Office of Administration, and the White House Operations section, which manages interns, travel, visitors, and photography. This office determines who gets which office, who can eat in the WH Mess, and who receives such tools as a minipager.

Executive Residence Usher's Office

This office manages the 92 people who serve in and maintain your family's personal quarters. This office has a digital locator box that flashes the location of each member of the FF when they are in the public areas of the WH.

Executive Clerk

The Executive Clerk handles all original copies of official documents that you sign, including laws, vetoes, executive orders, proclamations, and pardons. This office delivers sealed copies of messages from the president to either house of Congress.

Office of the First Spouse

The Chief of Staff to the First Spouse is in charge of implementing any agendas directed by the First Lady/Gentleman.

White House Curator

The White House Curator inventories and cares for the more than 14,000 pieces of furniture, china, silver, and artwork in the WH considered of historic value.

The Cabinet

The Cabinet is an advisory committee that functions at the pleasure of the president. The custom dates back to President George Washington's administration. Your Cabinet is composed of the heads of 15 executive departments, the secretaries of:

- Agriculture
- Attorney General
- Commerce
- Defense
- Education
- Energy
- Health and Human Services
- Homeland Security
- Housing and Urban Development
- Interior
- Labor
- State
- Transportation
- Treasury
- Veterans Affairs

In addition, most Cabinets include the:

- Chief of Staff to the President
- Director of Central Intelligence
- Chairman of the Council of Economic Advisers
- Counselor to the President
- Administrator of the Environmental Protection Agency
- Director of the Office of National Drug Control Policy
- Administrator, the Small Business Administration

- U.S. Representative to the United Nations
- U.S. Trade Representative
- Vice President of the United States

Cabinet meetings last from 15 minutes to three hours or more. Your Chief of Staff will determine the seating arrangement, although it's useful for you to sit in the middle of the long end of the conference table, with the sunlight pouring in the windows behind you. You may appoint a Secretary of the Cabinet to ensure orderly meetings and prompt follow-up to issues addressed by the Cabinet. Participants sit in comfortable black leather chairs at a large conference table in the Cabinet Room. Black coffee and water are essential refreshments. You may serve pastries, cookies, or other snacks, at your discretion.

Stars and Stripes Forever

The design of the Stars and Stripes has significant symbolic importance:

- Red: the blood shed in the defense of our nation
- Blue: pride in our nation
- White: purity of our nation
- 13 stripes: the original 13 colonies
- 50 stars: the 50 states

Essential Presidential Knowledge
How to Read the Insignia of the Joint Chiefs

As commander in chief, you will rely at times on the collective military wisdom of the Joint Chiefs of Staff. The JCS is led (under your direction) by the JCS Chairman and the JCS Vice Chairman, both typically chosen from among the country's generals.

- Other members include the Chief of Staff of the Army, the Chief of Naval Operations, the Chief of Staff of the Air Force, and the Commandant of the Marine Corps.

- The chairman is the principal military adviser to the president, the Secretary of Defense, and the National Security Council (NSC).

Here's how to tell them apart by their insignia:

Joint Chiefs of Staff

Military Insignia

	Collar	Shoulder	Sleeve
Admiral of the Navy	✮✮✮✮		
	Collar and Shoulder	Shoulder Marks	Shoulder Strap
General of the Army	✮✮✮✮		
	Collar and Shoulder		
General of the Marine Corps	✮✮✮✮✮✮✮✮✮✮		
	Collar and Shoulder	Shoulder Marks	
General of the Air Force	✮✮✮✮		

Military Chain of Command Flowchart

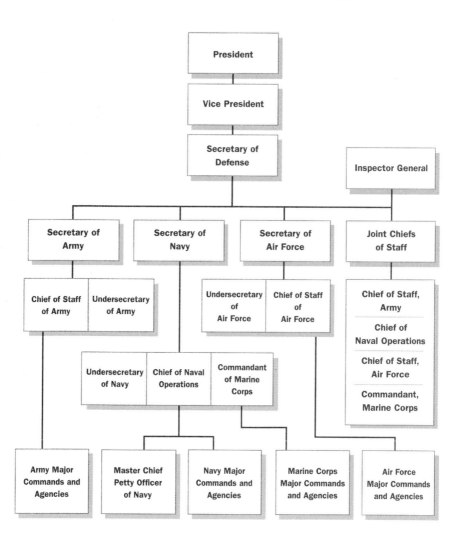

The Plum Book

Immediately following each presidential election the United States Office of Personnel Management publishes a book titled *United States Government and Policy Positions.* Although no one seems to remember why, this book is popularly called the Plum Book.

- It identifies 7,000 job positions in the executive and legislative branches of the federal government according to title, agency, type of appointment, and pay level.

- You may download this essential book from the Internet.

Salutations

Everyone, including the FS, should refer to you as "Sir," "Mr. President," "Madam President," or "The President" when in public.

Essential Presidential Knowledge

How to Remember People's Names

- Pay attention when you meet someone. Make a point of listening to their name.

- When you are first introduced to someone, use their name several times when talking to them. For instance, say, "Hi, Julia, so nice to know you," or "It's great to meet you, Julia," or "Julia, what a lovely sweater."

- Dissect the person's name in conversation, such as by asking, "Stephen–is that with a 'ph' or a 'v'?" or "Do you like to be called Suzie or Suzanne?"

- Take the first letter of the new person's name and combine it with the first letter of the name of the person who introduces you. Combine those initials, and the link may help you remember the names.

- If a person has the same name as a famous person or a close friend, try to associate them with that person.

- When you hear someone's name, imagine it as it would appear on his or her letterhead, because that mental image might stick with you better.

The White House Kitchen

- With 5 full-time chefs, including a pastry chef, and approximately 20 part-time staff, the White House kitchen prepares all meals for the president and FF.

- The WH kitchen is responsible for preparing state dinners and is able to serve dinner to as many as 140 guests and hors d'oeuvres to more than 1,000.

- Each year, the WH kitchen staff members dye thousands of eggs for the annual Easter Egg Hunt.

Frequently Asked Questions

How do I get snacks? Every refrigerator in the WH, including private quarters, offices, and public dining areas, including the Oval Office kitchen, is stocked with free sodas from the Coca-Cola and Pepsi-Cola companies.

• M&Ms, in special boxes decorated with the Presidential Seal, other candies, and various types of potato chips and pretzels are also donated free to the WH, and you may consume as many of these snacks, without charge, as you wish.

• Every day at 5:00 p.m. the WH Mess serves French fries to those working in the West Wing, and on Fridays the fries are accompanied by frozen yogurt studded with crushed Oreos.

• You must pay for any other snack food items that you keep in your personal quarters.

May I take pens and other office supplies back to my private quarters? Since much of your work will be conducted in your personal quarters, feel free to take office supplies back with you to the Executive Residence.

White House Mess

The WH Mess is a dining facility in the basement of the White House, open to certain WH staff members.

• Windowless and decorated with paintings of ships, the WH Mess is operated by the U.S. Navy, which is obligated to ensure that the president has food, no matter where in the world he is.

- The mess does not accept money and charges everything to personal accounts. Not every staff member is allowed to have an account, and there is much jockeying for the right to charge meals. Your administration determines who will and will not get this right.

- While your administration has no such obligations, historically, any person with a "blue" West Wing access pass has been eligible for an account in the WH Mess. Senior staff members with other types of passes also generally have accounts in the WH Mess.

- Among those who qualify for accounts, some have the right to eat in the mess, and others are only allowed take-out privileges. "Eat-in" account holders may invite outsiders to join them at a table.

Ordering Out

Most area take-out restaurants will deliver lunch to the WH. Ask for it to be delivered to 1600 Pennsylvania Avenue NW, service entrance. The guard will notify your secretary when your food arrives, and will arrange for it to be delivered to your desk.

- The establishments listed on page 60 are recommended restaurants in the immediate area of the WH. Any restaurant you choose will have to be vetted by the SS. Check with your security detail for further instructions.

Take-Out Map of Central Washington, D.C.

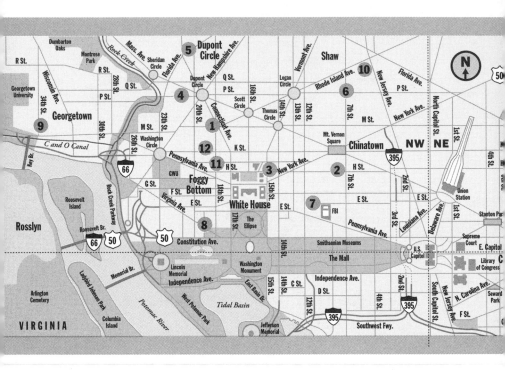

1. Acropolis
1337 Connecticut Ave. NW
Washington, D.C. 20036
202-912-8444

2. Alex Fish Market
709 H St. NW
Washington, D.C. 20001
202-544-1173

3. American Deli
818 15th St. NW
Washington, D.C. 20005
202-682-0811

4. Beduci Restaurant
2100 P St. NW
Washington, D.C. 20037
202-223-3824

5. Best Hunan Restaurant
2020 Florida Ave. NW
Washington, D.C. 20009
202-986-1333

6. D.C. Wing House
1509 7th St. NW
Washington, D.C. 20001
202-667-9461

7. La Baguette
901 E St. NW
Washington, D.C. 20004
202-347-6500

8. Panda
1807 West Virginia Ave. NW
Washington, D.C. 20002
202-526-8478

9. Philadelphia Pizza Co.
1201 34th St. NW
Washington, D.C. 20007
202-333-0100

10. Pupuceria Maria
2915 14th St. NW
Washington, D.C. 20001
202-291-3400

11. Sandwich World Shop
18001 I St. NW
Washington, D.C. 20006
202-737-1340

12. Sushi Express
1990 K St. NW, Lobby 7
Washington, D.C. 20006
202-682-0811

Sample Schedule for the POTUS

2410 HRS: THE PRESIDENT WENT FROM THE BOWLING ALLEY TO THE SECOND
FLOOR RESIDENCE. HE WAS ACCOMPANIED BY MR█████████, A PARTNER WITH
THE█████ LAW FIRM, ATLANTA, GEORGIA.

2430 HRS: THE PRESIDENT RETIRED.

0600 HRS: THE PRESIDENT RECEIVED A WAKE-UP CALL FROM THE WHITE HOUSE
OPERATOR.

0633 HRS: THE PRESIDENT WENT TO THE OVAL OFFICE.

0717 HRS TO 0720 HRS: THE PRESIDENT TALKED WITH THE FIRST LADY.

0730 HRS TO 0830 HRS: THE PRESIDENT PARTICIPATED IN A BREAKFAST MEET-
ING WITH THE VICE PRESIDENT, THE SECRETARY OF STATE, AND THE ASSISTANT
FOR NATIONAL SECURITY AFFAIRS.

0830 HRS: THE PRESIDENT RETURNED TO THE OVAL OFFICE.

0810 HRS TO 0855 HRS: THE PRESIDENT MET WITH MR█████, A PARTNER
WITH THE█████ LAW FIRM, ATLANTA, GEORGIA.

0920 HRS TO 0925 HRS: THE PRESIDENT MET WITH THE SECRETARY OF ENERGY.

0925 HRS TO 0927 HRS: THE PRESIDENT MET WITH HIS ASSISTANT FOR
DOMESTIC AFFAIRS AND POLICY.

0931 HRS: THE PRESIDENT WENT TO THE CABINET ROOM.

0931 HRS TO 0936 HRS: THE PRESIDENT PARTICIPATED IN A SIGNING CEREMONY
FOR A HOUSE BILL.

0936 HRS: THE PRESIDENT RETURNED TO THE OVAL OFFICE.

0940 HRS TO 0945 HRS: THE PRESIDENT MET WITH HIS PRESS SECRETARY.

0950 HRS TO 1000 HRS: THE PRESIDENT MET TO DISCUSS A MINING LABOR
DISPUTE WITH THE SECRETARY OF LABOR, THE SPECIAL REPRESENTATIVE FOR
TRADE NEGOTIATIONS, AND HIS CHIEF SPEECHWRITER.

1000 HRS: THE PRESIDENT RETURNED TO THE ROOSEVELT ROOM.

1000 HRS TO 1030 HRS: THE PRESIDENT MET TO DISCUSS THE LABOR DISPUTE
WITH INDUSTRY EXECUTIVES.

1030 HRS: THE PRESIDENT RETURNED TO THE OVAL OFFICE.

1115 HRS TO 1120 HRS: THE PRESIDENT MET WITH ████████ REGARDING THE
LABOR DISPUTE.

1121 HRS TO 1122 HRS: THE PRESIDENT MET WITH THE PRESS SECRETARY.

1130 HRS TO 1150 HRS: THE PRESIDENT MET WITH THE CHAIRMAN OF THE
COUNCIL OF ECONOMIC ADVISERS.

1153 HRS: THE PRESIDENT RETURNED TO THE SECOND-FLOOR RESIDENCE.

1159 HRS: THE PRESIDENT TALKED WITH HIS ASSISTANT, ████████

1235 HRS: THE PRESIDENT HAD LUNCH WITH THE FIRST LADY AND ████████

1312 HRS: THE PRESIDENT RETURNED TO THE OVAL OFFICE.

1334 HRS TO 1405 HRS: THE PRESIDENT MET WITH SENATOR ████████
THE PURPOSE OF THE MEETING WAS TO DISCUSS SENATOR ████████'S
RECENT VISIT TO THE PEOPLE'S REPUBLIC OF CHINA (PRC).

1405 HRS: THE PRESIDENT RETURNED TO THE ROOSEVELT ROOM.

1405 HRS TO 1425 HRS: THE PRESIDENT MET TO DISCUSS HUMAN RIGHTS,
URBAN POLICY, AND NUCLEAR DISARMAMENT WITH REPRESENTATIVES OF THE
NATIONAL COUNCIL OF CHURCHES OF CHRIST OF AMERICA.

1435 HRS: THE PRESIDENT RETURNED TO THE OVAL OFFICE.

1500 HRS: THE PRESIDENT MET TO DISCUSS THE LABOR DISPUTE WITH:
SECRETARY ████████ AMBASSADOR ████████
DEPUTY ASSISTANT MR. ████████

1551 HRS: THE PRESIDENT RETURNED TO THE SECOND-FLOOR RESIDENCE.

1554 HRS TO 1707 HRS: THE PRESIDENT TALKED WITH THE FIRST LADY.

1707 HRS: THE PRESIDENT RETURNED TO THE OVAL OFFICE.

1713 HRS: THE PRESIDENT WAS TELEPHONED BY MR. ████████ THE CALL
WAS NOT COMPLETED.

1720 HRS TO 1725 HRS: THE PRESIDENT MET WITH MR. ████████

1725 HRS TO 1740 HRS: THE PRESIDENT MET WITH AMBASSADOR ████████

1745 HRS TO 1750 HRS: THE PRESIDENT MET WITH MR. ████████

1806 HRS TO 1807 HRS: THE PRESIDENT TALKED WITH SECRETARY ████████

1810 HRS TO 1815 HRS: THE PRESIDENT MET WITH MR. ▓▓▓▓▓

1820 HRS TO 1822 HRS: THE PRESIDENT MET WITH MR. ▓▓▓▓▓

1822 HRS: THE PRESIDENT WAS TELEPHONED BY SECRETARY OF DEFENSE ▓▓▓▓▓ THE PRESIDENT'S SPECIAL ASSISTANT FOR APPOINTMENTS TOOK THE CALL.

1824 HRS TO 1825 HRS: THE PRESIDENT TALKED WITH THE FIRST LADY.

1834 HRS: THE PRESIDENT WENT TO THE OFFICE OF HIS ASSISTANT ▓▓▓▓▓

1834 HRS TO 1840 HRS: THE PRESIDENT PARTICIPATED IN A MEETING TO DISCUSS THE LABOR DISPUTE.

1840 HRS: THE PRESIDENT RETURNED TO THE OVAL OFFICE.

1841 HRS: THE PRESIDENT RETURNED TO THE SECOND-FLOOR RESIDENCE.

1844 HRS: THE PRESIDENT AND THE FIRST LADY WENT TO THE BLUE ROOM.

1844 HRS TO 1854 HRS: THE PRESIDENT AND THE FIRST LADY HOSTED A RECEPTION FOR FORMER CAMPAIGN WORKERS FROM NEW HAMPSHIRE. THE RECEPTION WAS HELD ON THE ANNIVERSARY OF THE PRIMARY IN NEW HAMPSHIRE.

1854 HRS: THE PRESIDENT WENT TO THE OFFICE OF THE VICE PRESIDENT.

1856 HRS: THE PRESIDENT RETURNED TO THE OFFICE OF MR. ▓▓▓▓▓

1856 TO 1900 HRS: THE PRESIDENT CONTINUED HIS MEETING TO DISCUSS THE LABOR DISPUTE.

1901 HRS: THE PRESIDENT WENT TO THE PRESS BRIEFING AREA. THE PRESIDENT MADE A STATEMENT TO THE PRESS ON THE TENTATIVE SETTLEMENT OF THE LABOR DISPUTE.

1907 HRS: THE PRESIDENT AND THE FIRST LADY RETURNED TO THE SECOND-FLOOR RESIDENCE.

1907 HRS TO 1958 HRS: THE PRESIDENT AND THE FIRST LADY CONTINUED TO GREET GUESTS ATTENDING THE RECEPTION FOR FORMER ▓▓▓ CAMPAIGN WORKERS FROM NEW HAMPSHIRE.

1915 HRS TO 1917 HRS: THE PRESIDENT TALKED WITH HIS ASSOCIATE FOR CONGRESSIONAL LIAISON.

1958 HRS: THE PRESIDENT RETURNED TO THE SECOND-FLOOR RESIDENCE.

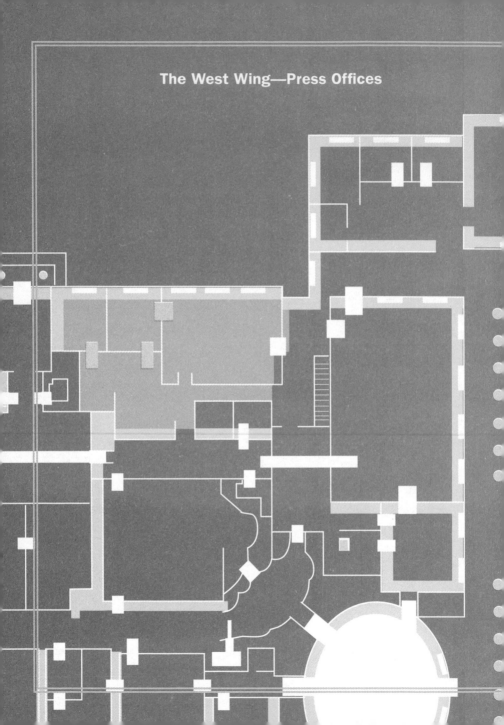

The West Wing—Press Offices

CHAPTER FOUR

GETTING SERIOUS—DEALING WITH CRISES AND THE PRESS

The forces at work in the modern White House are many and varied. The president must at all times remain in control, collected, and calm. The receiving and disbursal of information is a technically and emotionally challenging job in the WH environment, where media and other information gatherers are constantly challenging and confronting the executive mission. As president, you must master crucial skills such as information designation, joke telling, and data sharing. And you must learn when to simply walk away.

Essential Presidential Knowledge
The Situation Room

When problems, disasters, or national emergencies occur, expect to relocate to the Situation Room, a small, unprepossessing West Wing room with dark wood paneling, projection screens, and a massive conference table.

- Most Situation Room meetings last several hours, with military and political officials outlining their concerns and hopes regarding "situations" the government might be encountering.

- During such meetings, you may leave to use the bathroom whenever necessary, but otherwise are expected to pay close attention. Coffee, water, and, possibly, snacks will be readily available.

The Situation Room

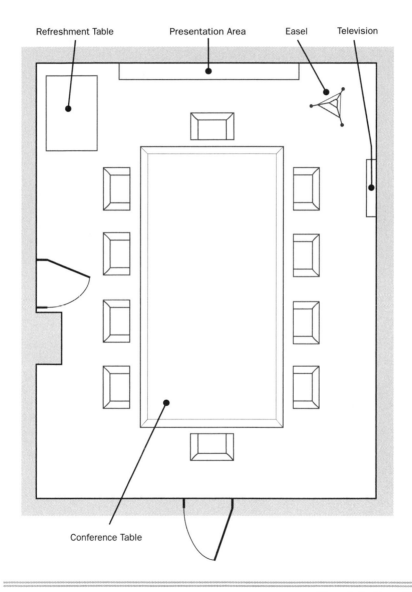

Refreshment Table   Presentation Area   Easel   Television

Conference Table

Essential Presidential Knowledge
Press Conferences

White House press conferences generally occur once a month or more, but you may change that schedule to suit your temperament and desires. Formal news conferences are usually announced at least one day in advance and take place at night in the East Room of the WH.

• Reporters covering the WH sit in folding chairs; you face them from a podium decorated with the Presidential Seal.

• You control the press conference, including choosing which reporters are allowed to ask questions.

• Traditionally, the correspondents who have covered the WH the longest are chosen to ask the first questions, but again, this is your call.

• Some reporters will ask simple, direct questions. Others will "speechify," extending their questions unnecessarily to give the networks enough time to scroll their names on the screen during the live broadcast.

• You may answer at length, or move on to the next question (see "Ten All-Purpose Answers to Tough Questions," page 72).

• Press conferences generally take between 20 and 40 minutes, including opening remarks.

Essential Presidential Knowledge
How to Act in a Press Conference

Comportment

- Relax. Practice beforehand the answers to likely questions. This will help you appear more confident.

- Speak slowly. Typically, people talk faster than normal while being interviewed on television. Consciously work at slowing yourself down.

- Speak clearly in a normal tone. The microphones will take care of the rest.

- Use proper grammar and avoid slang and off-color words.

- Speak to your questioner as though he or she were a friend. Be polite and kind.

Appearance

- Stick to plain colors and patterns. Cameras don't read polka dots and bold stripes well. Blue, brown, and gray fabrics are safe bets.

- Lighter-complected people should wear lighter colors but avoid bright white clothing, including white shirts. Off-white, yellow, and blue work best.

- Wear formal dress, such as a suit and tie, for interview programs. More casual clothes work well in "field" interviews, such as on your boat or while touring a natural disaster.

- Use a makeup base to cover freckles, dark circles, and blemishes, which will be highlighted by the camera. Do not use heavy makeup.

- Studio lights will reflect off gold and silver jewelry in an unflattering way, so avoid it.

How to Deliver a Joke

- Know your material: nothing ruins a joke like a flubbed line.

- Know your audience: nuns will respond differently from steelworkers to the same joke.

- Don't appear too eager to tell the joke. Just let it slip.

- Don't laugh at your own joke until the audience has started laughing.

- If one joke fails, let the humor pass for a while. Don't immediately try to correct your lapse in humor with another joke.

- Avoid ethnic, religious, and sexual humor of any kind.

- Self-deprecating humor almost always wins people over to your side.

Essential Presidential Knowledge
Information Designation to the Press

You must state before you speak whether any information is off the record, background, or deep background. Otherwise it will be assumed to be on the record.

On the Record
This is officially released information and makes up the bulk of WH news. Usually it is available to all press people, although occasionally on-the-record information will be released only to one news organization. Once it is published or broadcast, other news organizations may report it.

Off the Record
Officially, reporters are not allowed to report any information that is given to them "off the record." However, in practice, reporters often mention "off the record" talks to their editors or other reporters, who then publish or broadcast the information. This technically doesn't violate the meaning of "off the record." But you should be aware that anything you say can, and probably will, be publicized.

Background
This information must not be attributed to any one person. Thus the frequent use by reporters of the term "senior White House official."

Deep Background
You tell the reporter to be even more general in his attribution, crediting the information to, for instance, "an administration source" rather than a "senior White House official."

Essential Presidential Knowledge
Ten All-Purpose Answers to Tough Questions

- "No comment. Next."

- "That's a very interesting question, and one that merits further thought."

- "We are working on that issue as we speak."

- "Given the complexities of this ongoing issue, I would prefer not to address that in detail at this time."

- "I see you've been doing your homework. I'll turn that question over to the experts."

- "I'll be sure that someone from my staff gets back to you on that very good question."

- "I believe that we've said all we need to say on that subject. Thank you."

- "Thank you. Next."

- "You guys in the press ask the most interesting questions. I'll have to get back to you. Next."

- "I'm sorry, we don't have time for follow-ups. Next."

How a Teleprompter Works

- Your speech is typed into any word processing program and then fed into teleprompter software.

- You stand in front of a Plexiglas lectern that is see-through from the audience's perspective, but mirrored from your perspective.

- A flat monitor below the lectern, at the level of your feet where your audience can't see it, "plays" your speech.

- You are able to see your words reflected in the mirrored surface.

- This makes it possible for you to read your text while maintaining eye contact with your audience, without appearing to be using notes.

- An operator controls the pace of the words appearing on your lectern, so that they match your cadence. The result: you look professional, polished, and sincere.

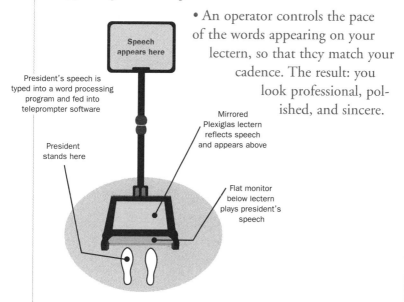

Speech appears here

President's speech is typed into a word processing program and fed into teleprompter software

Mirrored Plexiglas lectern reflects speech and appears above

President stands here

Flat monitor below lectern plays president's speech

How to Survive the Speech If the Teleprompter Fails

Prepare for this event by always keeping a paper copy of your speech at your side, so that you can read from that.

- Develop a sudden cough or hiccup that requires you to step away from the podium to clear up the problem, giving your technicians time to repair the teleprompter.

- Acknowledge that the teleprompter has failed, and appear relaxed until it is repaired. Smile and say, "Of course, I can't memorize every word of every speech."

- Take out a paper copy of the speech.

- Ad-lib. The press and the public generally respond well to genuine thoughts and emotions.

- When all is lost, postpone your talk.

Essential Presidential Knowledge

How to Release a Difficult News Item

If your administration has difficult or potentially embarrassing news to release, it's best to let the press know late on a Friday afternoon, when there is likely to be less coverage.

- The public pays less attention to news that is printed or broadcast on Saturday.

- If you have more than one difficult story, it's best to release the stories in a bundle, so that no particular story receives undue focus.

The Presidential Seal

The Presidential Seal is hung on the podium only when the president is speaking, never when another person is speaking. A military staff member is responsible for placing the seal on the president's podium just before he

speaks, and removing it immediately after he speaks.

The State of the Union Speech

The annual State of the Union speech is ranked among the president's most important public appearances. Your speechwriter will do dozens of drafts of the speech for you, based on meetings with you and other staff members.

- You'll begin by establishing themes for the speech, and then move on to specific details and anecdotes.

- Each part of your administration will comment on each draft of the speech over a period of several weeks prior to your address to the people. Then you will rehearse your reading of the speech (which might change up to the last minute, based on current events) so that it goes smoothly for Congress and the television cameras.

- It's recommended that you get a good night's sleep before the speech, have a snack before entering the Senate floor, and dress conservatively.

- The FF will be expected to attend, as will all of your friends and political enemies in Congress. Offer handshakes all around.

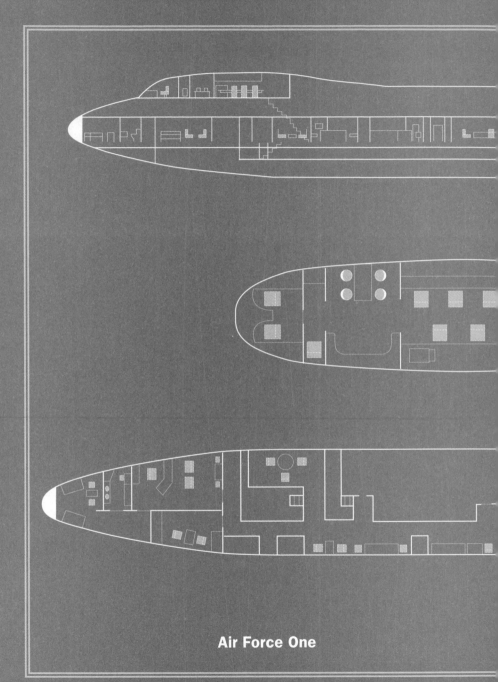

Air Force One

CHAPTER FIVE

GETTING AROUND—TRAVEL, SAFETY, AND SECURITY

Presidents travel well and often. Often the travel is for work, or combines work and play. But no matter where you go, you will travel in the utmost luxury and will never have to make a reservation or inquire as to local conditions or weather. Your staff will take care of all these issues. Wherever you go, an entourage of hundreds, at least, will follow. There will be counter-snipers on roofs, chefs in Winnebagos, and press spokespeople at every turn.

The Secret Service Vision and Mission

Vision Statement
"Building on a Tradition of Excellence and Meeting the Challenges of the Future."

Mission Statement
"The United States Secret Service is mandated by statute and executive order to carry out two significant missions: protection and criminal investigations. The Secret Service protects the President and Vice President, their families, heads of state, and other designated individuals; investigates threats against these protectees; protects the White House, Vice President's Residence, Foreign Missions, and other buildings within Washington, D.C.; and plans and implements security designs for designated National Special Security Events. The Secret Service also investigates violations of laws relating to counterfeiting of obligations and securities of the United States; financial crimes that include, but are not limited to, access device fraud, financial institu-

tion fraud, identity theft, computer fraud; and computer-based attacks on our nation's financial, banking, and telecommunications infrastructure."
from The Department of the Treasury

The Secret Service

• 125 offices worldwide

• 2,100 special agents

• 1,200 uniformed officers

• 1,700 other staff members

• $1.05 billion annual budget

• Uniformed officers protect the WH complex, the vice president's residence and foreign embassies and missions in the Washington, D.C., area. They operate magnetometers, serve as counter-snipers and canine handlers, and maintain special operation posts.

• Agents go through an initial 9-week training course about law and investigative techniques, followed by an 11-week course in advanced protection, including weapons training, emergency medicine, water survival skills, and evasive driving techniques.

• Agents regularly attend classes on the latest security techniques to update their skills.

• Agents participate in simulated crisis training exercises called "Attack on Principal," which mimic real-world situations.

• The SS will protect you and your spouse up to 10 years after you leave office, if you desire.

- Protection of a spouse ends after a divorce.
- Will protect your children until age 16.
- Agents receive continuous advanced training during their time with the agency.
- In the forefront of cyber-security prevention and response.
- Agents are not allowed to discuss any aspect of their work.

Frequently Asked Questions

Do I have to use my SS agents? Yes, for your own safety, and for the good of the country, you have to use your agents at all times. You will have a permanent detail of special agents assigned to protect you. When you travel, an advance team of SS agents will survey the site to be visited. They will determine the manpower, equipment, hospitals, and evacuation routes to be used in case of emergency.

How do they protect me? Traditionally, the SS has tried to envelope the president in a 360-degree circle of safety, with agents boxing in the president at all times in public. However, a new methodology is being developed that assesses threat levels, using intelligence and historic precedence, to determine the appropriate level of coverage for a given situation.

Who are those guys on the roof of the White House? In public, you will never be out of sight of SS agents. When you leave the White House, you might notice SS snipers on the roof. When you golf, SS agents will be combing the fairway and examining the greens.

Essential Presidential Knowledge
SS Code Names

These top-secret code names have been used at various times by the SS:

Acrobat/Andy: Andrews Air Force Base

Bamboo: Presidential motorcade

Baseball: Secret Service Training Division

Birds-eye: Department of State

Bookstore: White House Communications Center

Cactus: Camp David

Cement Mixer: White House Situation Room

Cobweb: Vice President's office

Magic: Helicopter coordination command post

Pacemaker: Vice President's staff

Playground: Pentagon helicopter pad

Pork Chop: Old Senate Office Building

Roadhouse: Waldorf Astoria hotel, New York City

Angel/Cowpuncher: Air Force One

Wheels Down: Air Force One has landed

Air Force One

The designation Air Force One doesn't apply to any one particular plane. Rather, it is the moniker for any plane in which the president is flying. In practice, however, you will usually fly in one of two specially configured Boeing 747-200B aircrafts with the tail numbers 28000 and 29000, respectively. Some facts:

• The planes can be refueled in flight.

• There is an executive suite with a stateroom (including dressing room, lavatory, and shower) and the president's office.

• There is a combination conference/dining room.

• There are separate bedrooms and sleeping areas for guests and security personnel and other staff members, and the news media.

• Two galleys are capable of serving 100 meals at a sitting.

• There are six passenger lavatories, including disabled access facilities.

• Each plane is 231 feet, 10 inches long (the length of a city block), 63 feet, 5 inches high (taller than a 5-story building), with a wingspan of 195 feet, 8 inches.

• Interior wiring is specially coated to resist the electrical force of a thermonuclear blast.

• The planes travel at a top speed of 630 miles per hour, to a ceiling of 45,100 feet. They have a range of 7,800 miles when fully fueled.

• They have a total capacity of 102 people, including a crew of 26.

Air Force One

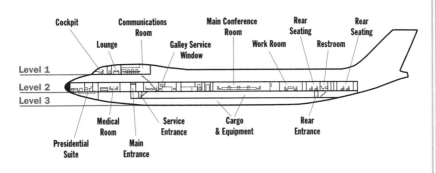

Cockpit · Communications Room · Lounge · Galley Service Window · Main Conference Room · Rear Seating · Rear Seating · Work Room · Restroom

Level 1
Level 2
Level 3

Presidential Suite · Medical Room · Main Entrance · Service Entrance · Cargo & Equipment · Rear Entrance

Level 1

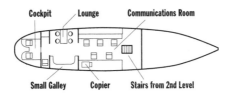

Cockpit · Lounge · Communications Room

Small Galley · Copier · Stairs from 2nd Level

Level 2

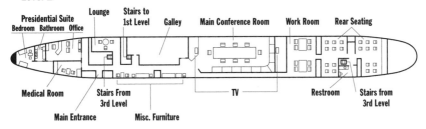

Presidential Suite: Bedroom Bathroom Office · Lounge · Stairs to 1st Level · Galley · Main Conference Room · Work Room · Rear Seating

Medical Room · Stairs From 3rd Level · Main Entrance · Misc. Furniture · TV · Restroom · Stairs from 3rd Level

Level 3

Service Entrance · Stairs to 2nd Level · Cargo & Equipment · Rear Entrance · Stairs to 2nd Level

- The planes have a perfect safety record and are widely considered to be the safest planes in the world.
- They are equipped with built-in antimissile devices and other defensive capabilities.
- You are allowed to sit in the cockpit during landing and takeoff.

The Presidential Motorcade

When the president travels by car, he typically is part of a motorcade that comprises some 27 vehicles, each of which may contain up to 5 people. (The vice-presidential motorcade generally consists of 16 vehicles, in a similar arrangement.)

Presidential Limos
- Protected by the SS, all motorcade support vehicles maintained by the WH Military Office.
- Based on Cadillac V8s, with clear glass windows.
- Transported by plane from location to location when you travel.

- Splinter-proof bullet-proof glass/polycarbonate windows, antiballistic steel panels in doors, floor, firewall, and trunk.

- Get about 10 mpg in the city.

- Offer heated leather seats, rear climate control, rear audio system, telephone, television, DVD-CD player, and individual cup holders for each passenger.

Security on the Road

When you travel, the SS will:

- Check every attic, closet, and crawl space of any building you are scheduled to enter.

- Decorate your hotel room with wired objects that, if bumped, would alert the SS to a problem.

- Arrange motorcades and map routes, and set up decoy motorcades to confuse would-be assassins.

- Note the routes to nearby hospitals.

- Block all streetlights, train crossings, and stop signs so that you don't have to stop. The president never has to experience traffic.

- Position defensive snipers on buildings.

- Identify and watch any locals who are considered to be security risks.

Presidential Motorcade

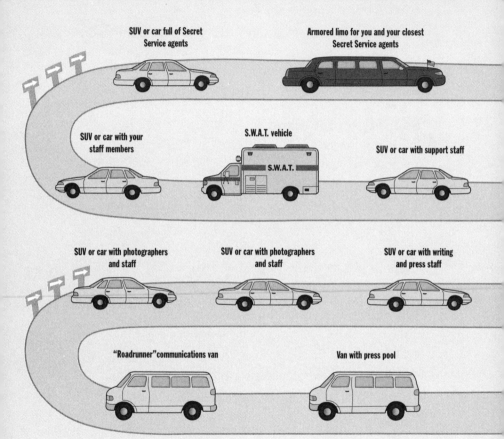

Marked police car with bomb-sweeping capabilities

SUV or car full of Secret Service agents

Armored limo for you and your closest Secret Service agents

SUV or car with your staff members

S.W.A.T. vehicle

SUV or car with support staff

SUV or car with photographers and staff

SUV or car with photographers and staff

SUV or car with writing and press staff

"Roadrunner" communications van

Van with press pool

Marked police car that maintains the integrity of the motorcade

Marked police car that maintains the integrity of the motorcade

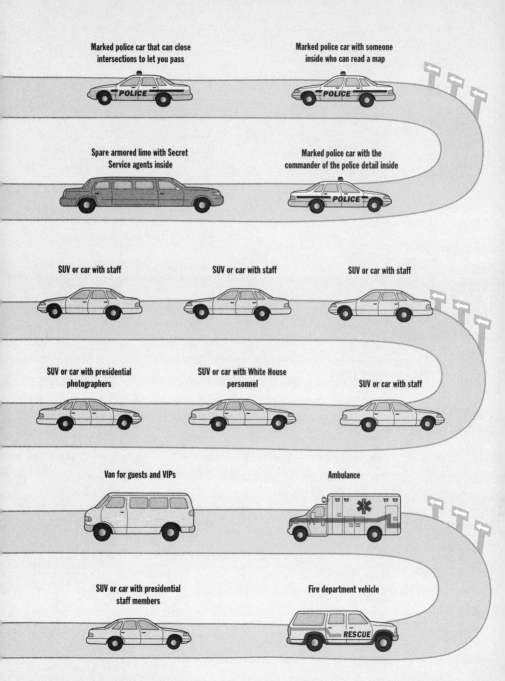

Essential Presidential Knowledge
Public Appearances

As president, you will average about 450 public appearances a year, in locations as diverse as the Lincoln Memorial and Angkor Wat.

- At each location you will face throngs of admirers and, sometimes, protestors, the press, and local dignitaries.

- Cameras will record your every word and handshake.

- You must appear to be accessible, yet also be protected from those who wish you harm.

- You must always be in reach of your national security command centers.

- Appearances require a massive amount of planning, with every moment of your journey programmed to the minute by the White House Advance Office.

- For each trip, this office begins four to eight weeks in advance to choreograph the activities of the Cabinet, Communications Office, Scheduling Office, Press Office, Secret Service, speechwriters, motor pool, and others. Together, they formulate the message to be conveyed on the trip and choose the locals that will best convey this message; and they examine local calendars and agendas, plus information sources such as *The Farmer's Almanac*, to find events and celebrations that the president can appear at.

- The Intergovernmental Affairs and Political Affairs Offices will suggest local dignitaries, such as mayors and congresspeople, who will appear alongside the president.

- This office will also highlight issues that should be addressed or avoided according to local sensitivities.

- The SS will coordinate its activities with its local office. The White House Communications Agency will assemble a mobile satellite station and erect your bulletproof podium, called "The Blue Goose."

- The Air Force will determine which local airport can accommodate Air Force One, and will in advance transport the two presidential limousines (the one you will ride in as well as a decoy), vehicles for the SS, the "Roadrunner" communications van, and a Marine One presidential helicopter.

- The WH advance team will arrive at the site about six days ahead of your arrival, to complete a checklist of perhaps 500 to-do items, ranging from placing tape markers to choosing the appropriate music to locating the best spots for you to greet the public. The SS will diagram the motorcade and approve the driver of each vehicle.

- The "storyboard" of the event will be drawn up, showing where the president will walk, where he will stop, and where he will eat and sleep. Satellite time will be reserved to assure press coverage.

- A "crowd builder" will publicize the event locally to assure that there is a good audience for each appearance. This person will work with the local hosts to distribute handbills in grocery bags, on people's doors, lying right-side up on the sidewalk, and taped to mirrors in public restrooms.

Bands, cheerleaders, and pom-pom people will be invited to perform. Banner-painting parties will be organized. Three thousand or so balloons will be inflated.

• The press will be accommodated with a separate tent equipped with phones, electrical outlets, and high-speed Internet access. There will be portable video-editing equipment and tables where several hundred people can write and file their stories. The day before the trip the White House Advance Office distributes a press schedule "bible" to reporters, outlining the trip, and makes its own, more detailed, schedule.

Frequently Asked Questions

Do I have to pack myself? The maids and butlers of the WH residence staff will pack your clothes for you. Let them know if you have any special needs or desires. Your bags will be conveyed to your destination, and your on-road valet will take care of unpacking your clothes and making sure they are cleaned and pressed.

International Appearances

International advance teams often arrive in the host country three months in advance because the team will have less information about a foreign local than an American local. If the president is to host a state dinner at the local embassy, about 150 White House place settings of china, silver, and serving pieces will be transported from Washington to the embassy, along with Navy chefs and stewards, as well as the food that will be prepared.

Essential Presidential Knowledge
Maintaining Your Profile

Dignity must be maintained at all times. According to the White House Advance Manual: "The President must never be allowed into a potentially awkward or embarrassing situation, and the advance person is sometimes the only one who can keep that from happening. . . . For example, an oversized cowboy hat, a live farm animal, an Indian headdress, or a Shriner's 'Fez' could produce a decidedly unpresidential photograph. Common sense must be used to make sure that the dignity of the office of the President is never compromised by the well-intentioned generosity of local partisans."

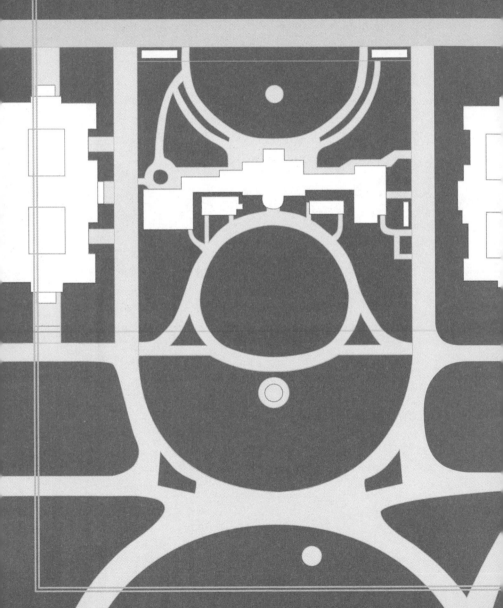

CHAPTER SIX

GETTING OUT—OFFICIAL
CEREMONIAL FUNCTIONS

The president's evening hours are often given over to formal state dinners honoring one dignitary or another. You will be required to attend state performances, cocktail parties, balls, and other social functions—some for the sake of the country, some for the sake of re-election. Every person who visits the WH expects special treatment, and generally the president gives it. You will shake hands with thousands and become friends with hundreds during your time in the WH. This chapter describes how to attend and navigate such functions.

Diplomatic Reception Room

This is where you'll most commonly greet important guests, such as diplomats. Personal friends also often use this entrance.

• This room was originally the furnace room for the WH. It is oval-shaped, with antique wallpaper showing American scenes, such as Niagara Falls.

• This is the room where Franklin Roosevelt held his fire-side chats.

• Guests enter this room after exiting their cars at the porte cochere.

State Dining Room

Used only for formal government functions, the State Dining Room on the northeast corner of the second floor has walls paneled in hand-carved oak, with Corinthian pilasters and a frieze, painted off-white.

Main Ceremonial Areas of the White House

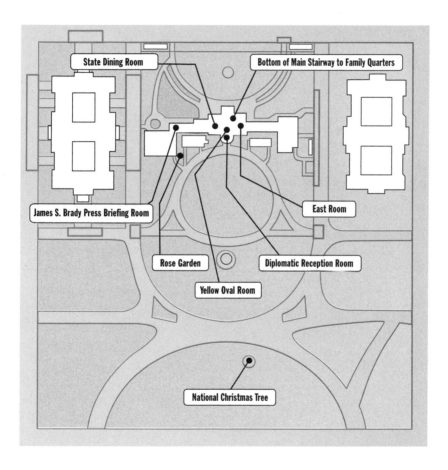

State Dining Room

Bottom of Main Stairway to Family Quarters

James S. Brady Press Briefing Room

East Room

Rose Garden

Diplomatic Reception Room

Yellow Oval Room

National Christmas Tree

- A George P. A. Healey oil portrait of Abraham Lincoln hangs above the fireplace.

- Carved into the mantelpiece is a quote from President John Adams, commemorating his first day in the White House: "I pray Heaven to bestow the best of blessings on this house, and on all that shall hereafter inhabit it. May none but honest and wise men ever rule under this roof."

- The high-ceilinged room has the capacity for 80 guests seated at 10 round tables, or up to 102 guests seated at one massive horseshoe-shaped table and one long rectangular table.

- During recent administrations, the round-table configuration has been the preferred seating arrangement. Each place setting has a service plate, napkin, place card, menu, three knives (fish, dinner, salad), three forks (fish, dinner, salad), and four glasses (water, white wine, red wine, champagne).

- While the specifics depend on the food being served, during the meal each guest will be given a dinner plate, salad plate, dessert plate, finger bowl, cup and saucer, dessert fork, dessert spoon, demitasse spoon, and any specialty utensils such as a fish fork or steak knife.

- At most state dinners you will be expected to raise a glass and make a toast to at least one visiting foreign dignitary. Your speechwriter can help with this.

Menu

Grilled Halibut, Bay Scallop Risotto and Lobster Sauce,
served with Shafer Chardonnay "Red Shoulder" 2001

❋

Roasted Rack of Lamb,
Wild Mushrooms and Armagnac Sauce

❋

Sweet Potato Flan and Autumn Vegetables,
served with Soter Pinot Noir "Beacon Hill" 1999

❋

Avocado and Heirloom Tomato Salad
with Toasted Cumin Dressing

❋

Arabica Ice Cream and Coffee Liquor Parfait
Caramelized Banana and Pineapple
served with Honig Sauvignon Blanc "Late Harvest" 2002

Sample State Dinner Menu

Hail to the Chief

The song "Hail to the Chief" is traditionally played when the president arrives at an official ceremony or formal occasion. Some presidents have chosen not to have it played at certain functions.

- The song is intended to give the president time to proceed in a stately way to the center of activities and draw the audience's attention.

- The music was composed by an Englishman, James Sanderson, for the lyrics of Sir Walter Scott's poem, *The Lady of the Lake*, for a performance on the London Stage.

- Later, Albert Gamse wrote these lyrics for when the music is played for the President of the United States:

Hail to the Chief we have chos-en for the na-tion,

Hail to the Chief! We sa-lute him, one and all.

Hail to the Chief, as we pledge co-op-er-a-tion

In proud ful-fill-ment of a great, no-ble call.

Yours is the aim to make this grand coun-try grand-er,

This you will do, that's our strong, firm be-lief.

Hail to the one we se-lect-ed as com-mand-er,

Hail to the Pres-i-dent! Hail to the Chief!

[Repeat]

Paying for Official Parties

The Social Secretary and the Chief Usher must determine the financial arrangements for all official functions. For instance, a state dinner for a foreign dignitary will be paid for by the Department of State.

- At times you and the First Spouse will host an event, but it will be paid for by an outside organization, and that group will be billed and charged penalties for late payments.

- Political events sponsored by your political party's national committee must be paid for in advance. This is the only type of function that must be paid for in advance. Congress instituted this policy following a series of late payments for political functions in the late 1990s.

The White House Art Collection

The White House contains more than 450 valuable artworks and objects, many of them donated by previous presidents. The art on display includes:

- *Liberty*, by Constantino Brumidi

- *Morning on the Seine*, by Claude Monet

- *A Western Landscape*, by Albert Bierstaddt

- *A Portrait of Theodore Roosevelt*, by John Singer Sargent

- *Nocturne*, by James McNeill Whistler

- *1897 Morning on the Seine, Good Weather*, by Claude Monet

- *Bear Lake, New Mexico*, by Georgia O'Keefe

- *Young Mother and Two Children*, by Mary Cassatt

White House Events and Traditions Attended by the President

A partial list of events, in calendar order:

- African-American History Month: Reception for prominent African Americans in the WH

- Presidents' Day: A visit to the Lincoln Memorial

- Little League Baseball Day: Host the champions, throw a few balls

- White House Grounds and Garden Tour: Public tour of gardens. You may make a welcoming speech if there is time

- Easter Egg Roll: You and the FF will be expected to attend and mix with the children

- Spring Garden and Grounds Tour: The public is invited to visit the grounds of the White House. You may make a welcoming speech if there is time

- Ceremony Honoring Youth T-ball Players: President is expected to hit a ball off the T with a bat

- October Fall Garden and Grounds Tour: See Spring Garden and Grounds Tour, above

- Veterans' Day White House Tour: Visit Arlington National Cemetery. Lay wreath at Tomb of Unkown Soldier

- Lighting of the White House Christmas Tree: Flick the switch to turn on the lights

- Mobility Disabled Tour: People in wheelchairs and with other mobility disabilities may tour the White House. President may make welcoming speech if there is time

- Senior Citizen Holiday Tour: Senior citizens are invited to tour the White House and see the holiday decorations. President may make welcoming speech if there is time

- Christmas Candlelight Tour: The public is invited to visit the White House to see the holiday decorations. President may make welcoming speech if there is time

The White House Easter Egg Hunt

- The first White House Easter Egg Hunt took place in 1878.

- Traditionally the largest public celebration of the year at the White House, it is attended by the president's extended family and numerous children under age six.

- Tickets are distributed free to the public on a first-come, first-serve basis.

- The egg-rolling race, based on a 19th-century Washington-area Easter tradition, was introduced to the White House celebration, using spoons from the White House kitchen, in 1974.

- "Bunny" is usually a White House staffer dressed in an Easter Bunny costume. Ursula Meese, the wife of President Ronald Reagan's attorney general, Edwin Meese, so enjoyed the costume that she served as Bunny during six egg hunts and earned the sobriquet "The Meester Bunny."

Essential Presidential Knowledge

How to Tie a Bow Tie

While your valet is always available to help you prepare for formal occasions, there are times when you'll want to dress yourself:

1. Arrange bow tie loosely around your neck.

2. The end held by your left hand should be one and a half inches longer than the other end.

3. Wrap the longer end over the shorter end and bring it up through the loop.

4. Make the front part of the bow by doubling the short end behind the collar points.

5. Use the thumb and forefinger of your left hand to hold the loop. Drape the long, loose end over the front of this bow.

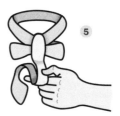

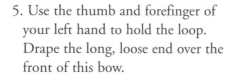

6. Use your right forefinger to push the hanging end up behind the front loop and poke it through the knot. Pull the ends of the bow to tighten and even it.

Essential Presidential Knowledge

How to Deal with Language Barriers

Even in this day and age there are world leaders who do not speak English well. However, you do not need to learn their language in order to communicate with them about important issues.

• The State Department will provide you with any translators necessary, with security clearance, at any time of the day or night.

• You will speak into the telephone, and your translator will repeat your statement in the appropriate language on another telephone. Then the world leader will respond in his or her language, and the statement will be translated back to you.

• Problems can occur when the other world leader wishes to have his or her translator translate your statements. When this occurs, use both translators to avoid misstatements of fact.

Essential Presidential Knowledge
How to Do the Box Step

Ceremonial dinners and celebrations often include ballroom dancing, and you will be expected to take a turn.

• Begin by facing your partner with your shoulders parallel.

• The man places his right hand just below the woman's shoulder blade, fingers together, elbow pointing slightly to the side.

• The woman's left arm should rest on the man's upper arm, with her thumb along the inside of his arm, fingers over his shoulder.

• The woman's right hand rests in the man's left palm, held at the shorter partner's eye level.

• To avoid stepping on your partner's feet, position yourself one-half of your body width to the left of your partner, with your right foot between your partner's feet. This will help you avoid foot injuries.

Proper Stance

Basic Box Step

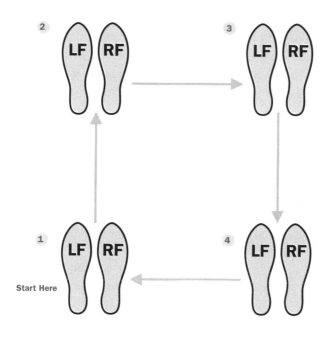

- The basic box step:
  (Quickly, and light on the feet)
  Right foot forward
  Bring left foot to meet right foot
  Right foot to the right
  Bring left foot to meet right foot
  Right foot back
  Bring left foot to meet right foot
  Left foot to the left
  Bring right foot to meet left foot

Essential Presidential Knowledge

How to Shake Hands

Handshakes probably grew out of the need for medieval Englishmen to demonstrate to each other that they were not holding a weapon. Now the convention has spread around the world. While many people judge a person by the style of handshake he or she offers, the handshake says less about a person's character than about his or her ability to learn how to shake a hand. The handshake is composed of three components:

Extension

- Extending with your palm down suggests that the other person is in the underdog position.

- A vertical offering of the palm suggests a cooperative spirit.

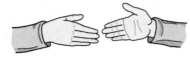

- Offering your palm up suggests you are at the other person's service.

Pressure

- In the West, a "strong" handshake suggests strength of character.

- In many other parts of the world, it would be considered impolite, or even sexually suggestive, to squeeze strongly. When in doubt, squeeze firmly, but gently.

Duration

- Duration and the number of pumps varies widely from country to country. Generally, if you like someone, hold their hand longer and pump it more times.

- Holding the hand longer than is comfortable is often a method of intimidation.

Meeting Celebrities

If there's anyone you'd like to meet, ranging from a pop diva to the national toad-calling champion, just notify the office of the Social Secretary. Presidential invitations are rarely declined.

Frequently Asked Questions

How do I know how to act with people from different cultures? You may take any questions you have regarding how to act, or how others should act in your presence, to the Office of Protocol. This office "advises, assists, and supports the president on official matters of national and international protocol, and in the planning, hosting, and officiating of related ceremonial events and activities for visiting heads of state."

Essential Presidential Knowledge

How to Place Your Hand Over Your Heart

- Using your right hand, remove your hat, if you are wearing one.

- Hold it at your left shoulder so that your hand extends over your heart on the left side of your chest.

- If you have no hat, place your right hand, with the palm open, over your heart.

- Leave your hand on your heart until the conclusion of the anthem.

Essential Presidential Knowledge
How to Salute

1. Raise your right hand sharply so that the tip of your forefinger touches your right eyebrow (or, if you are wearing a hat, touches your headgear just to the right of your right eye).

2. Keep your arm (shoulder to elbow) parallel to the ground at about 45 degrees forward from your body.

3. Keep your thumb and fingers joined, palm to the left, with your hand and wrist straight.

4. Keep your back erect and alert.

5. Turn your head and eyes toward the person or object you are saluting. Do not turn your head toward your hand.

6. Drop the salute smartly to your side in one motion. Do not slap your side.

Tips

• You are expected only to return a salute, not initate it—you are the commander in chief of the military, and those lower in rank will initiate the salute.

• Never have an object in your mouth or right hand when saluting.

• Salute the flag when it is six paces away from you and hold the salute until it has passed six paces beyond you.

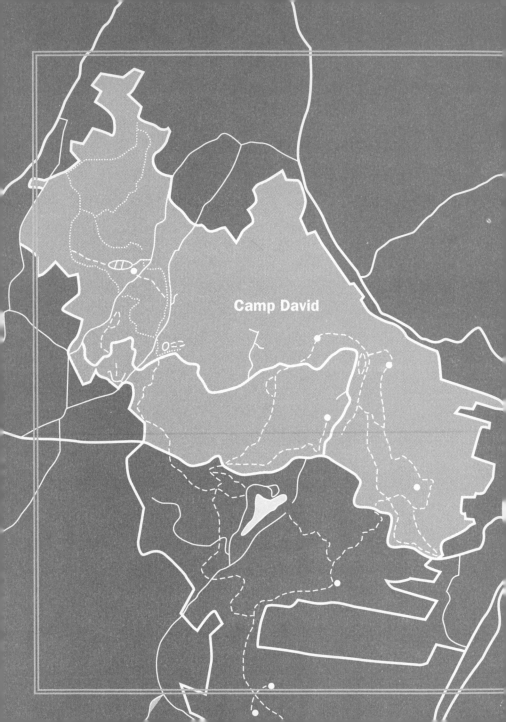

CHAPTER SEVEN

GETTING AWAY FROM IT ALL— PRESIDENTIAL REST AND RECREATION

There are certain private areas within the WH where the president and FF can escape the hustle and bustle of life in the nation's capitol. The WH has wonderful recreational opportunities, from swimming to jogging and, of course, horseshoes. However, every president needs to take a break once in a while, to escape the demands of the WH and get some fresh air. As president, you are free to use Camp David, in Maryland, for weekend getaways. Most presidents also frequently return to their home states for visits.

White House Recreational Facilities
Movie Theater

The movie theater is in the east colonnade. The front row seats are La-Z-Boy Recliners, and the remaining 61 seats are also quite comfortable. There is a popcorn machine, and standard movie snacks and drinks are available. At your request, the Motion Picture Association of America will deliver any first-run feature for you to watch.

Swimming Pool

President Franklin D. Roosevelt constructed the original WH swimming pool in 1933 because he suffered from weakness caused by polio and needed to swim to strengthen his upper body. In 1969, President Richard M. Nixon filled in the pool to make additional room for the White House Press Corps. President Gerald R. Ford, an avid swimmer, immediately ordered construction of a new, outdoor pool, after taking the oath of office. In 2002, President George

W. Bush installed solar panels to heat the pool. The pool is available for lap swimming, water polo, and other activities 24 hours a day.

Horseshoe Pit
President George H. W. Bush had the first horseshoe pit installed at the White House. It is located near the swimming pool.

Bowling Alley
In 1947, a group of well-wishers paid to install a two-lane bowling alley in the basement of the WH for President Harry Truman's 63rd birthday. At the time, President Truman had not bowled a single frame since he was 19 years old. Many succeeding presidents have made frequent use of the bowling alley. President Nixon was known for bowling alone. President Carter often took guests to the bowling alley. In 1950, the White House bowling league was established, sanctioned by the American Bowling Congress. Teams were formed by the SS, the domestic staff, the gardeners, the secretaries and telephone operators, and others. Following September 11, 2001, however, the bowling league was disbanded, although the lanes are still available for use by the president and his guests.

Camp David

If you'd like to head to Camp David or elsewhere early on Friday, begin to make your arrangements Thursday afternoon. Just tell your chief of staff to make sure everything is ready for your departure, and it will be ready.

Camp David

- It's located in Maryland's Catoctin Mountain Park.
- The park was created in 1936 as part of the Works Progress Administration.
- The present site of Camp David was chosen as a presidential retreat in 1942, when the SS became concerned about the possibility of a German U-boat attack on the yacht *Potomac*, which President Franklin Roosevelt used to escape Washington's muggy summers.
- The property was named "Shangri-La" by President Roosevelt, who intended to use it just during World War II.
- President Dwight D. Eisenhower renamed the property "Camp David," after his grandson, in 1953.
- It's still part of the Catoctin Mountain Park, but not open to the public.

Frequently Asked Questions

May I take guests to Camp David? Yes, it's common for the First Family to invite guests to Camp David for the weekend.

Is there a charge for guests? No.

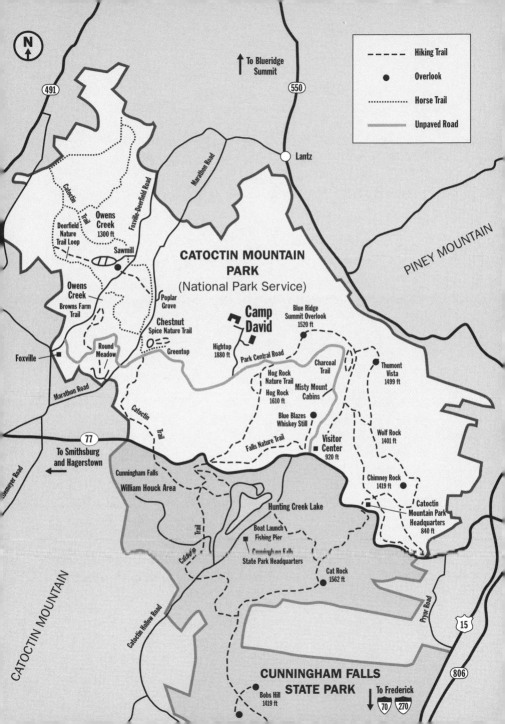

Essential Presidential Knowledge
Recreational Attire

Do's
- Military flight jacket embroidered with Presidential Seal and your name
- Gimme cap
- Jeans and cowboy boots
- Golf clothes of any kind (except shorts)
- Running and gym shorts (only when performing these activities)
- Running shoes
- Slacks
- Polo shirts
- Chambray or plaid shirts
- Hunting jacket
- Tennis clothing

Don'ts
- Shorts, except specifically for exercise
- Sandals (women may wear dress sandals)
- Sarong
- Suits
- Business shoes
- Dark socks

Quiet Time
As president, you'll never be alone in public, but you can find privacy in your WH living quarters. SS agents won't automatically follow you into your personal quarters on the WH second floor, nor will they monitor your movement from room to room in your private quarters (as they would in the public areas of the WH). They will be stationed at the entrance points to your WH private quarters.

Presidential Sleepovers

At your discretion, official and unofficial guests may stay in your personal quarters. Or you can put them up at Blair House, the official presidential guest quarters, located across Pennsylvania Avenue from the White House. Your guests will not be charged.

Marine One

The Marine One designation applies to any helicopter on which the president is a passenger. The most commonly used helicopter is the Sikorsky UH-60 Black Hawk, first developed in 1974 as an Army troop transporter. The president generally uses an updated, luxury VIP version called the VH-60N. Marine One includes such features as:

- Energy-absorbing landing gear meant to help passengers survive crashes.

- Self-sealing puncture-resistant fuel tanks that minimize explosions and fires.

- Protective armor (on the VH-60N) that can withstand attacks by 23 mm shells.

- A crew of 4 and room for 8 passengers.

- A maximum speed of 180 mph and a range of 445 miles.

- A length of 64 feet and a height of 16 feet, 8 inches.

APPENDICES

Terms of Employment

Employment Contract
From *The U.S. Code Sec. 101—Commencement of term of office*
> "The term of four years for which a President and Vice President shall be elected, shall, in all cases, commence on the 20th day of January next succeeding the day on which the votes of the electors have been given."

From *The U.S. Constitution, Section 1, Amendment 20 (1933)*
> "The terms of the President and Vice President shall end at noon on the 20th day of January . . . and the terms of their successors shall then begin."

Termination of Employment
Your job is secure unless impeachment proceedings are brought against you by the Congress. The term *impeachment* applies only to the initial indictment against you, which is followed by a trial by the House of Representatives. The law is covered by six clauses in the U.S. Constitution: Article I, sections 2 and 3; Article II, sections 2 and 4. These direct that the House of Representatives indicts the president, the Senate tries him, and the Chief Justice of the United States presides over the inquiry. The House will draw up the articles of impeachment, including specific charges, and present the case to the members of the Senate, who are sworn in as jurors. Impeachable charges include "Treason, Bribery, or other high Crimes and Misdemeanors."

Only three presidents have ever faced a real danger of being removed from office by impeachment.

You may quit by simply tendering your resignation to the Secretary of State.

Compensation

From *The U.S. Code Sec. 102—Compensation of the President*
    "The President shall receive in full for his services during the term for which he shall have been elected compensation in the aggregate amount of $400,000 a year, to be paid monthly, and in addition an expense allowance of $50,000 to assist in defraying expenses relating to or resulting from the discharge of his official duties, for which expense allowance no accounting, other than for income tax purposes, shall be made by him. He shall be entitled also to the use of the furniture and other effects belonging to the United States and kept in the Executive Residence at the White House."

Raises

From *The U.S. Constitution, Article 2, Section 1, Clause 7*
    "The President shall, at stated times, receive for his services, a compensation, which shall neither be increased nor diminished during the period for which he shall have been elected, and he shall not receive within that period any other emolument from the United States, or any of them."

However, Congress can approve a raise for your successor.

Vacation

The president may take as many vacation days as he or she desires. Often, a president's time off is called a "working vacation." For perspective, here are the average vacation habits (including travel time and "working vacation" days) away from the White House of recent presidents:

George W. Bush, 98 days a year

William J. Clinton, 19 days a year

George H. W. Bush, 135 days a year

Ronald Reagan, 41 days a year

Jimmy Carter, 19 days a year

Retirement

The president's pension kicks in the day he or she leaves office. The amount is based on a formula tied to the salaries of Cabinet Secretaries and varies depending on what Congress has approved for those positions. One recent president received about $160,000 a year, with cost-of-living increases, and could earn more than $7,000,000 over the course of his retirement, if he lives to be 80 years old. In addition, you will have a $96,000-a-year staff allowance, plus free rent on any office you choose to rent anywhere in the United States. The SS will protect you and the First Spouse for 10 years after leaving office, if you desire. Presidents who are forced out of office by impeachment do not receive retirement benefits. If you were to resign before or during an impeachment proceeding, you would receive benefits.

Guide to Common U.S. Government Acronyms

ARTS
National Endowment for the Arts

CEA
Council of Economic Advisers

CEQ
Council on Environmental Quality

CIA
Central Intelligence Agency

CNS
Corporation for National and Community Service

DHS
Department of Homeland Security

DOC
Department of Commerce

DOD
Department of Defense

DOE
Department of Energy

DoED
Department of Education

DOI
Department of the Interior

DOJ
Department of Justice

DOL
Department of Labor

DOT
Department of Transportation

EPA
Environmental Protection Agency

EXIM
Export-Import Bank of the United States

FEMA
Federal Emergency Management Agency

GSA
General Services Administration

HHS
Department of Health and Human Services

HUD
Department of Housing and Urban Development

HUMANITIES
National Endowment for the Humanities

IMLS
Institute of Museum and Library Services

NASA
National Aeronauts and Space Administration

NSF
National Science Foundation

OMB
Office of Management and Budget

ONDCP
Office of National Drug Control Policy

OPIC
Overseas Private Investment Corporation

OPM
Office of Personnel Management

OSTP
Office of Science and Technology Policy

PC
Peace Corps

PRC
Postal Rate Commission

SBA
Small Business Administration

SSA
Social Security Administration

STATE
Department of State

TDA
Trade and Development Agency

TREAS
Department of the Treasury

USAID
United States Agency for International Development

USDA
United States Department of Agriculture

USTR
Office of the United States Trade Representative

VA
Department of Veterans Affairs

WH
White House

Additional Sources

The following sources can be accessed for further information:

Books
Bohn, Michael K. *Nerve Center: Inside the White House Situation Room.* Brasseys, Inc., 2003

Buckland, Gail, and Kathleen Culbert-Aguilar. *The White House in Miniature: Based on the White House Replica by John, Jan, and the Zweifel Family.* New York: Norton, 1994

Joynt Kumar, Martha, and Terry Sullivan. *The White House World: Transitions, Organization, and Office Operations.* Texas A&M University Press, 2003

Truman, Margaret. *The President's House: A First Daughter Shares the History and Secrets of the World's Most Famous Home.* New York: Ballantine, 2003

Walsh, Kenneth T. *Air Force One: A History of the Presidents and Their Planes.* New York: Hyperion 2003

Whitcomb, Claire, and John Whitcomb. *Real Life at the White House: 200 Years of Daily Life at America's Most Famous Residence.* New York: Routledge, 2002

Newspaper and Magazine Archives (among many)
The Chicago Tribune
The Detroit Free Press
The New York Times
The Washington Post
Washington Monthly

Websites
http://www.access.gpo.gov
http://www.americanpresident.org
http://www.amvets-ny.org
http://www.askthewhitehouse.gov
http://www.beyondboooks.com
http://www.dtic.mil
http://www.edition.cnn.com
http://www.elks.org
http://www.emperor.vwh.net
http://www.factmonster.com
http://www.fas.org
http://www.gi.grolier.com/presidents
http://www.high-impact-leaders.co
http://www.infoplease.com
http://www.nationalgeographic.com
http://www.news.bbc.co.uk
http://www.presidentialpetmuseum.com
http://www.usnewswire.com
http://www.whitehouse.gov
http://www.law.cornell.edu/uscode/

Index

Note: Italic page numbers indicate illustrations.

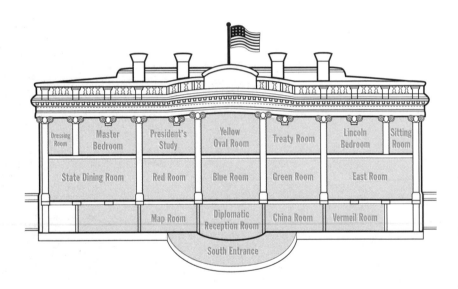

Dressing Room

Master Bedroom

President's Study

Yellow Oval Room

Treaty Room

Lincoln Bedroom

Sitting Room

State Dining Room

Red Room

Blue Room

Green Room

East Room

Map Room

Diplomatic Reception Room

China Room

Vermeil Room

South Entrance